THE CREATIVE'S CURSE

TODD BRISON

Copyright © 2016
Todd Brison.
All Rights Reserved.

No part of this publication may be reproduced, distributed, or transmitted in any form or by any means, including photocopying, recording, or other electronic or mechanical methods, or by any information storage and retrieval system without the prior written permission of the publisher, except in the case of very brief quotations embodied in critical reviews and certain noncommercial uses permitted by copyright law.

First Printing 2019
First Edition 2019

10 9 8 7 6 5 4 3 2 1

THE
CREATIVE'S
CURSE

TABLE OF CONTENTS

FOREWORD 1
   Jon Westenberg 1

DISCOVERY 5
   And So It Begins 6
   What's your story? 9
   Questions of doubt to slay as you start your journey 12
   Don't get stuck in this lie: 18
   The Message is Greater than the Medium 20
   Tag. You're It. 23
   Do Both 25
   Concerning the Teasing of Your Friends 28
   11 Things You Will Fear When You Decide to Start 30
   10 Ways to Come Up with More Ideas 31
   Just say "it's for work" 37
   Learn Everything 39
   Here's the Big Secret… 41

DISCIPLINE 43
   Guess who gives you permission to create? 44
   Every single creative struggles with discipline. 46
   Priorities 51
   Discipline Tool #1 – The Free Time Checklist 55
   Discipline Tool #2 – Micro Journaling 60
   One Question 64
   2 Ways to March Your Way Into Recognition 66
   Dear Person Stifling Creativity at Your Job 71
   This is the Middle of the Book 73
   Blink 75

Excuses 78
The Ultimate Guide to Beating Creator's Block 79
  Beating Creator's Block Step 1: Figure Out Why Your Block is (Really) Happening 79
  Beating Creator's Block Step 2: Build Creative Triggers . 84
  Beating Creator's Block Step 3: Finding Flow at the Drop of a Hat 90
  Beating Creator's Block Step 4: Lies the Brain Tells 97
The Answer is No 102
The Weird and Wonderful Characteristic Most People Don't Have 104

DESTINY 110
Here's the thing 111
The 6-step guide to selling your soul for money 114
There will be days you don't want to get out of bed 119
How to Be Creative in a Non-Creative Role 120
Not-So-Magic Tactics; Magic Results 123
Don't BS just because you can 131
The Creative vs. The Businessman 133
The Success Monster Part 1 - What to do After Your Post Goes Viral 135
Break the Rules 138
The Success Monster Part 2 - Until You Connect, You Are Nobody 140
Read these words whenever the momentum slows 143
The Success Monster Part 3 - The Irony of Creative Victories 144
"Your work doesn't appeal to everyone" 146
The Success Monster Part 4 - What Happens After Your Dreams Come True? 147
You Will Never Hear These 4 Words Enough 152

Love. Feel. Cry. 155
For the things that are impossible to capture: 157
Maybe 159

ACKNOWLEDGEMENTS 161

NOTES AND SELECTED FURTHER READINGS 163

ABOUT THE AUTHOR 164

ONE LAST THING... 165

FOREWORD
JON WESTENBERG

I hit a milestone the other day.

I'm now at around 100,000 words published on Medium.

That's a lot, any way you look at it. I figured it was time for one of those posts, you know - *"This is what I've learned from publishing 100,000 words."*

The thing is, when I sat down to write that post, it felt like a waste of time. It would suggest that I have a clue what I'm doing.

And I really don't.

I'm full of doubt, I'm full of worry and panic, and I'm struggling with the direction I'm moving in.

Here's something people ask me a lot: *"How do I know that being a writer and an entrepreneur is 'The Dream' I'm meant to be following?"*

That's a great question, and I totally get why people ask it. After all, that's the kind of question I would have desperately been seeking an answer to a few years ago.

TODD BRISON

I used to look for my calling, a lot. You hear from so many people who will tell you about the moment when they realized their life's calling and committed themselves to following that at all costs. It's normally pretty specific. You know these people - the ones who realized they had to be singers when they had an epiphany on a mountain top, and they love telling everyone about it.

I struggle with this all the time. There are so many things I want to do. I want to draw comic books, and write prose, and create art installations—but equally, I want to grow businesses, and explore being an entrepreneur.

When people email me to ask me how I knew what I wanted to do and who I wanted to be, I have to explain that they've got the wrong idea. The way the question is phrased, it pushes me to question whether or not I know, *who, what and why I am.*

I know it seems like I must be incredibly together, because I get a lot of things done and I write a blog that gets a lot of views—but the reality is, on any given day, I only know three things about myself:

I am a blogger

THE CREATIVE'S CURSE

I am an entrepreneur

I am a creative.

If that seems vague, that's because I've never been able to maintain a strong hold on any more detailed idea of who, what and why I am. I've never been able to define myself in some visionary way.

I have no real idea where the hell I'm going to be in 10 years, and if I told you I did know you'd be well within your rights to call me on it as a liar.

There's such a clash, with these different areas of interest, these different things that I desperately want to do. Finding a way to marry them becomes incredibly difficult and daunting.

There's no key to getting over that struggle. There's no magic spell, no "One Weird Trick."

I've never wanted to give away any of these parts, these interests and passions and ideas that make me who I am. And I still don't. As my career progresses, I'm getting more and more caught up in the world of business and entrepreneurship. It's something I've been involved in for the past 10 years, and I love it.

Up until the past few months, I've been constantly dealing with a state of panic, asking myself if I'm compromising who I am by not taking the time to fully explore all of my passions, asking myself if I even know who I am.

When I read Todd's book, I had an instant connection with it. He's written beautifully about the struggles of doubt and direction I face every day, the conflict all of us who call ourselves creatives must battle against. Page by page, his work sums up what it means to make art, and how it affects us.

The Creative's Curse doesn't try to be a magic wand. It's a guide, it's going to walk next to you on the journey.

Sometimes, that's enough.

Discovery

The first cave artist was most likely bludgeoned with a big stick for not contributing.

Before we go too far down this road, remember your curse is a luxurious one.

And So It Begins

It's not your fault, you know.

It's not your fault you started down this path. Odds are you were probably making up stories before you could talk. You never went anywhere without your trusty crayon.

And instead of buying your mother a card for her birthday, you decided it was a better idea to draw a masterpiece with crayons on the wall she'd just painted. (This story is purely hypothetical and not at all exactly what happened to me when I was four years old).

The truth is, you didn't choose the creative life. Admit it, there have been days when you wish you could just push the pixels aside, pass the pencil to someone else and do something worthwhile, like maybe construction or sales.

But you were not born for sales. You were not born for the assembly line or a cubicle or regular working hours. You probably weren't even born for a normal sleep schedule.

THE CREATIVE'S CURSE

As you progressed through your adolescence, you hung on to one core truth, one small but crucial aspect of your being which separates you.

You will always be a child.

In the back of your mind lives the young girl who used to dress up her dolls, the same one who built daisy crowns on the soccer field instead of tending to the goal. (Sports are temporary. Plant-based accessories last forever).

You reject button-pusher mentality. You combine ideas from the universe and create a new big, beautiful Frankenstein. You upset the status quo.

Because, after all, that's what a child does.

He displays absurd amounts of energy before crashing in a heap of disappointment and tired and cranky. He plays so aggressively you think he will explode. He learns where all the lines are (mostly so he can know when to cross them). He is violently curious, peering under every nook and cranny left unexplored.

He presents his discovery to the world, and even though they may have already seen it, they now look with a new light. Because adults forget the joy of ordinary things.

TODD BRISON

Children do not.

Give up on growing up.

It's not for you.

What's Your Story?

In 10th grade, when I was still good-looking, but not quite as good looking as I am now, we were given the assignment to write a poem for English class.

Most people jotted down the typical A/B rhyming scheme.

Some people really gamed the system and wrote haikus. (17 glorious syllables, almost zero effort).

Do you know what I wrote?

I wrote a freaking sonnet. 14 lines, each exactly 10 syllables. Every 2 lines rhymed. Apparently I had a lot of time on my hands back then.

But after I turned it in, everything changed.

Not only did the teacher enjoy the piece, he stood up the next day and read it in front of everyone. The room laughed at certain passages and Mr. Bone glowed at me, appreciating the "extra effort."

(It's funny. When you're doing what you love, "extra effort" doesn't feel "extra" at all.)

I remember the flutter in my stomach when he read my name.

I remember putting my head down, trying to pretend like I wasn't *loving* the attention.

I remember the pats on the back from my friends.

What I remember most happened afterwards.

The class dismissed, and between the pile of bodies flocking toward the door, the teacher pulled me aside between the backpacks, looked me in the eye and said:

"Your father was a great writer as well."

My gut dropped to the floor and my heart rocketed into the clouds. It was over. From that point, I could never *not* be creative.

That was my defining moment. I'm betting you have one too.

I often wonder if engineers go through something similar. Was there a moment when their whole future exploded with options because of an equation they solved? Or teachers? Were they the ones who coached people through ACTs not because they had to but because they felt a calling?

What about people who hate their jobs? Did nobody ever tell them they were special? Did nobody ever tell them they see the world in a way nobody else does?

Instead of applause, were all their ideas met with mockery?

I don't know much about the world, but I do know this:

You were meant for something.

Somewhere on this green earth is a not a job, but a calling which works for your exact cocktail of experiences, passion, and ability.

We need you to find it.

Questions of Doubt to Slay as You Start Your Journey

What if I am alone?
You will be. To go through a process you and only you will understand is to be alone.

You can and should expect support from people, but you shouldn't expect them to walk with you.

What if people don't get me?
They won't.

Nobody will get it. Not your mom, not your brother, not your boss.

And that's the whole point.

If they got it, they wouldn't need you.

The primary asset which sets the Creative apart is her ability to see a future nobody else sees.

People will question your vision all the way up until the point where you bring it into reality. (After which, everyone will say "I could have thought of that," but that's another topic for another time).

Don't explain what you're trying to do. *Do* what you're trying to do, and then let your art speak for itself.

What if I can't make it?
I honestly don't know if you can. I don't know if you're good enough. I don't know if you've got it in you.

But you owe it to yourself to find out.

What if I get stuck?
Let me tell you a little secret: getting stuck is part of the game. If you never get stuck, you aren't producing enough art.

At times, the Muse will withdraw. You'll show up to where you've met her before, and instead you will find emptiness.

The metal of every creative is forged in this valley. Each time you get stuck, you learn another way to get unstuck, wiggle out of the darkness, and dance once again.

What if being an artist makes me poor?
It could happen, but I hope not.

I say this online all the time and I'll address it more in this book - **I don't want you to be a starving artist**. Being poor sucks, and in this world of infinite connection, there's no reason to be.

More than that, though, you may need to take a look at what "poor" is.

How much money do you really need if you're doing what you love every day?

What if I never get famous?

Fame is a by-product of talent, work, luck, and time.

Let me say that again, this time in italics:

Fame is a by-product of talent, work, luck, and time.

Talent: Not necessarily what you're born with, but what you cultivate. It's your responsibility to foster whatever natural ability you have, and grow in those abilities.

Work: Showing up, every day. People with half the talent can win twice as much as they should just by out-working their peers

Time: Nothing is grown overnight. Most of the time, people get famous just by staying in the game longer than anyone else. Jordan Harbinger started the Art of Charm podcast before anyone else was doing it. 7 years later, he's quite the star.

Luck: When you're awake at 11 P.M. and someone sends you a message about doing custom work for them – that's luck (sort of). When you're exploring a new app, happen to mention what you do, and someone requests your service by the end of the week – that's luck (again, sort of).

Luck is one of those things which happens to people who are in the right place at the right time to *the right people*. Become the right person, and the right times and places generally find you.

A lot of Creatives start because we love the attention, but *more* attention is not always better. Fame is not always better.

Again, the goal should be building a lifestyle that lets you do what you love, however many people that includes.

Why do other people get attention, but I don't?
For now, just assume everyone who has a big platform deserves it.

One of the most poisonous lines of thought will tell you success is random, there's nothing you can do and life isn't fair.

All you can control is what you do. Comparison is a waste of time.

Create art. Create art. Create art. Everything else can fall where it may.

Do I suck?

Insecurity and doubt is a part of art. Besides, in such a subjective field of work, someone will always think you suck.

The true answer to this is "I don't know," so here are a few tips to knock the edge of the question:

1. Do the best you can. Nothing less. Pour all your ability, no matter how small or large, into your work.

2. Figure out how to get better. It's important this is kept completely separate from your published work. Few things destroy an artist's confidence quicker than trying to publish and learn simultaneously

Nirvana for a Creative is to create exactly *what* she means to, exactly *when* she means to. When you can do that, you won't suck.

Am I kidding myself?

No. If you're reading this book, it's likely you have some untapped creative potential. Unless you have zero self-awareness, you've got to see this through.

Don't allow anyone to tell you what you should feel about yourself.

Is any of this worth it?

Yes. Yes yes yes. The reward of a Creative is always worth the fight.

Better to go through a little discomfort finding yourself now than to live with a mountain of regret at the end of your life.

What's the point?
The point is to get to start finding and fostering your talent so you don't grow up an old, bitter could-have-been.

Too many people give up on the dream at 24, and trudge their way through the next 60 years where they die, happy to finally be released from a life of boredom.

Don't get stuck in this lie:

I can guarantee you this - if you sit behind a desk and try to come up with a sentence nobody has written before, you will be waiting a long, long, long time.

Thousands of Creatives (you may be one of them) stay stuck behind the hurdle of originality.

Instead, look to see how others have done things. Steal from them. Mercilessly and ruthlessly rip their ideas away and recreate them as your own. Then tear it up and start over.

Some people how to write by copying the Great Gatsby word for word. While that sounds mind-numbingly awful to me, the logic is sound. My first few attempts at writing a book were close to carbon copies of the Pendragon series.

It isn't plagiarism, it's just part of the process.

Steal. Destroy. Create.

And then do that over and over forever.

This is the Creative's Curse - you can never hope to come up with anything new. The best you can do is say:

"This is the truth, told as only I can tell it through my experiences, beliefs, and talents at this moment in time.

Now do you understand?"

The Message is Greater than the Medium

All I'd done was make a PowerPoint possible to sit through without wanting to kill yourself. The framing was awkward, the typography was bad, and the photos were stolen.

Why were people acting like it was a big deal?

Next I was asked if I could put together a poster.

"Sure, but I'm not a designer."

Next it was a video.

"I'm not a designer."

Soon, the outdated video software we were using wasn't enough to build what needed to be built. I asked for a few Adobe products.

"Just to get me started and to help out. But I'm not a designer."

I spent hours, days, weeks, learning animation through After Effects. Brushed up my Illustrator skills. Bought a Wacom tablet so I could draw (and I do not draw well).

"I'm not a designer"

What I made was clunky, awkward, and took me forever because I had to keep running to YouTube to figure out what I was doing. But I couldn't stop. I poured my heart, soul, and humor* into what I was creating.

(*I once created a presentation explaining proper headgear featuring a man with a cat on his head. Hilarious, right? Turns out the client was a branch of the federal government... and they weren't too thrilled*)

If I knew I wasn't a designer, and didn't particularly want to be a designer, why was I spending all my time learning all this designer-y crap?

Six months, seven animated videos, countless altered or created images, and three produced live shorts later, I finally realized what was going on.

I cared more about the message than I did the medium.

Even though it was unconscious at first, something inside me knew writing alone wasn't getting across the feeling, the instinct, or the action I wanted people to take away.

At the end of the day, *creation is about sending a message*. It's about the transfer of a thought or action or emotion.

Certainly focusing on one medium alone is the quickest way to become successful, but to develop a full creator's tool belt, it helps to become proficient at a lot of things.

By the way, you are allowed to do more than one thing. Don't let anyone tell you otherwise.

Public speaking (unless you do it poorly) is just another form of creation. I approach that and deploy it entirely differently than I would a blog post.

I still don't think I'm a designer.

But I do know better than to try and fit every message into one kind of box.

Tag. You're It.

Unless you attended school on Mars, I'm guessing you had a teacher who pushed you toward a "safe" career choice.

I've recently spoken with a friend who feels her daughter is being told "college is the only path."

It makes sense, you know. Public schools (like most machines) build a curriculum that will fit the largest amount of people, not every person. It's all a numbers game.

> *"Our test scores averages are up 10 points"*
> *"Our graduation rates have risen 22%"*
> *"More of our students are pursuing higher education"*

Understand this - **every single public school exists to answer to someone else.** They are organizations which take the lives and potential of young human beings and squeeze the data out of them. Living, breathing students turn into dots on a graph passed to state governments.

Public schools do not exist to mold young minds. Teachers might, but the school system? No way. The *actual* education of students takes a back seat in order to get metrics that work. Art is treated as filler in most schools because their board wants the curriculum to look well rounded.

Now that you're good and riled up, I'm going to flip the script.

It is **your** responsibility to move past all that. Part of the Creative's Curse is dealing with insecurity that came from your youth.

In order to step into your calling as a Creative, you have to give yourself permission to create junk. It's not going to be graded. It's not going to be tracked. It doesn't matter if it's the safe choice or not.

Just make new *stuff*. Make new stuff until the voice of Mrs. Sanders (or whatever that ogre you had in 6th grade was named) fades away.

Because you can't stifle this anymore. You need to create. You've denied it for too long.

Do Both

It could be you didn't go straight into the creative marketplace. Maybe you took a safe, secure job (just like I did), so you could pay bills, take care of your family, and not have to wonder where the next paycheck is coming from.

It could be, despite all of those noble things, you've become bitter with your employer (just like I did). Or worse, maybe you've become hopeless (just like I did).

It could be reading this book is just an escape, a chance for you to dream of the life you could have lived.

Whenever I talk to someone who feels their creative abilities are being stifled, I tell them about Hannah from New York.

Hannah is 16 at time of writing, and in a public school, which means her teachers, principals, and fellow students are all pushing her toward going to college.

But there's a problem - Hannah's a budding graphic designer. She isn't really sure college is the only choice anymore.

Let's take a look a potential scenario:

At 16 she decides college is a little too much of a commitment. She's going to double down on her current skill.

We can pretend Hannah lives in a fairly small town that has a small coffee shop. With no connections (or money), she could walk around, get a sense of what the shop is about, and draw a mock rebranding. She spends a couple months drawing up the ads, pictures, or posters, and presents them to the business owner.

Worst case scenario - the business owner says no. **Best case scenario** - the business owner loves the work, and asks if she can use it for the store.

If the owner says yes, Hannah's freedom from debt, obligations, and classwork comes in handy because *it does not matter if she gets paid.*

From ages 16-18, Hannah does unsolicited rebrands for every small business within 50 miles of her. Sometimes they say no, sometimes they don't. Sometimes she gets paid, sometimes she doesn't.

Here's the magic - at this point, she can STILL decide to go to college. Only now she has a) money saved, b) a portfolio, c) a direction for a career and d) *actual* experience in the field.

THE CREATIVE'S CURSE

I'd be willing to bet exactly zero of her classmates will have all four of these. Most won't even have one.

Instead of stifling her creativity and going to college OR risking it all on the talent she has, why can't she do both?

She could do both.

You can do both.

You may not have the financial freedom or the time Hannah has, but if it means enough to you, you'll find a way.

I adore my 9-5 because it gives me the financial freedom to do things for free, to work on my talent without the threat of bankruptcy. I'm going to build a whole side career (although it may take a little longer) without the gray hairs that come with "putting it all on the line"

The next time you're faced with a "this or that" situation, why not do both?

Concerning the Teasing of Your Friends

When you start down your creative path, it's going to be a mindset shift for both you and the people who know you.

They say:

"You're a different person"

And you'll have to realize you're actually the same person. You've just stopped denying your dreams.

They say:

"Do you think you're better than me?"

And you'll have to wrestle with that. DO you? I hope not.

They say:

"Look at our big shot Artist."

And you'll have to disregard the sarcasm.

They say:

"Aren't you Lisa's son?"

And you'll have to remember even a prophet is disregarded in his home town. Those who knew you at your youngest will take the longest to come around.

They say:

"Come out! You can't change the world in one night!"

And you'll have to remember that's true. BUT, you have to balance the investment you're making in them with the investment you're making in your future.

Invest comes from a root meaning "to make new" or to "give a new form."

Without investment, there is no new form.

They say:

"Who do you think you are?"

And you better be ready to give them an answer.

11 Things You Will Fear When You Decide to Start

You will fear running out of money
You will fear your parents' skepticism
You will fear your friends laughter
You will fear telling people your dream
You will fear making the wrong move
You will fear you don't have what it takes
You will fear other people's opinion
You will fear failure
You will fear success (weird isn't it?)
You will fear running out of ideas

But you will fear a cage the most. And that will keep you in the game.

10 Ways to Come Up with More Ideas

There is this myth in the creative community (probably because people like me use words like "Muse" and "Calling") that ideas simply strike out of the sky, and the Creative must merely act on them, rejecting all others when this mystical lady comes to call.

That's a poisonous way to think because you put your very livelihood in the hands of someone/thing else. *Reminder: you have command over your creative career.*

It also becomes way too easy to play the victim card ("I just haven't been inspired"), the procrastination card ("I've been tinkering with several ideas"), and/or the misunderstood card ("I can't explain how Creativity works to you, peasant").

It's tempting to say "Here are ways to never run out of ideas," but I won't. All the Internet hyperbole gets on my nerves. I *will* say "here are some ways I keep coming up with ideas." These have worked for me and so far, I'm still chugging.

1. Study art religiously.
Every artist in the universe has been inspired by other art. It's what we do. The Creative's conscious feeds off a collection of emotion brought to a tangible piece of work

Is it time for a comeback for a certain style of design? Does a sentence in your favorite novel inspire a separate train of thought? (I wrote nearly 1,200 words from one *sentence* in John Green's *Paper Towns*.) If you could change your favorite piece of art in one way, what would that way be?

Lots of ideas are simply other ideas plus or minus one element.

2. Walk. A lot.
Thoreau wrote an entire thesis on this which I'm not going to quote from because it's free and you can find it online anywhere to read yourself.

The body (including the brain) needs blood flow to exist. Walking increases the blood flow within the body, giving your brain a boost. I probably explained that wrong but I'm not really concerned about that because I'm not a scientist and neither are you. How 'bout we just leave it at WALKING IS MAGIC.

3. Study other people.

"People watching" is somewhere on my list of 101 Ways to Break Out of a Creative Rut, and I'm still sticking to it. Airports are one of my favorite places to do this. There are plenty of people to stare at and make up lives for. Try to figure out why they walk, talk, and act like they do. Paint their pain. Compare them to your own life. Other humans, whether by themselves or by their work, are an incredible way to inspire new work.

4. Go outside.

I'll often walk around the 20 square ft. park outside my office barefoot. It sounds pretty hippie-ish, but there seems to be something to the whole fresh air thing.

Besides, nature has been surviving for quite some time now, and it doesn't even go to Whole Foods. It's probably doing something right. (For more context, google "Earthing")

5. Be around kids.

The obvious caveat here is DO NOT WALK UP TO KIDS RANDOMLY AND TALK TO THEM. You will get arrested. Or at least some weird looks from parents.

But if you have a son or nephew or work at a children's camp, spend as much time around them as possible. Volunteer with Big Brothers, Big Sisters.

Kids are idea geniuses because there are no limitations to their imaginations.

Yet.

6. Look to your past.

This doesn't necessarily mean meticulously journaling. I'm not crazy about that, and have even developed Micro Journaling as an alternate practice. (We'll talk about that later)

But one of my most popular posts on Medium came from a random story I remembered from my childhood. A lot of times we're trying to look forward, trying to predict what the most popular thing to write about would be.

This is the wrong approach.

Artists need to reflect. Moreover, our own experiences are the *one thing* nobody else has. There's a gold mine in there, I promise.

7. Mind map.

I almost left this one out because I honestly don't use it that often. But I've done it at work a couple times and the results are straight magic. Google it if you haven't heard the term before.

8. Get outta town.
The mind, by design, assimilates and automates as many things as possible. I'm sure you've had the experience of driving an hour to work and having no memory of what happened on the way there.

The more our grey matter automates, the more it can devote itself to solving problems (like why we would want to watch a scary movie right before bed). But this automation backfires whenever our normal scenery, full of life and beauty and ideas, turns into white noise. Getting into a new area serves the double benefit of you having new things to explore AND it highlights what you love about your dwelling when you get back.

9. Dream.
I know, I know, you can't always control whether or not you dream. But you can control whether or not you take naps. Salvador Dali used to take naps, wake himself up, and then draw whatever he saw.

Worked out okay for him.

10. Go wide, then go deep.

In my Micro Journaling, I come up with several different ideas on one topic. I go wide to try and circle all the possibilities. Then the next morning I pick just ONE item from the previous day's list, and go deep - I list 10 other things that have to do with that thing. That's actually where the idea for this part of the book came from.

Running out of ideas is one of the biggest underlying fears of the Creative lifestyle.

These practices can help you stay away from that.

Just say "it's for work"

A funny thing happens when you start to (re)discover your creative side.

Your friends will say *"what are you doing?"*

And if for some reason you are a freak of nature with mounds of self-esteem and don't want to lie, you'll say:

> *"Oh, I'm just working on my (fill in creative passion here)."*

At this point, the person will say "Oh, okay" or something like that but it will come across more as an "Ahhh" and it will be laced with something between sarcasm and skepticism. It's exactly the response you give a five year old who just told you he's making mud pies:

> *"Wow! Look at you, little Jimmy!"*

That's the reaction you're getting.

Normal people (bless them) have been trained to think creativity is something fluffy. Like it's more a hobby than a habit and more a luxury than a requirement. They will laugh and file you in the same part of their brain as little Jimmy and his mud pies.

Luckily, I've found a secret around this, a way to avoid the condescending looks, the raised eyebrows, and the thinly veiled disbelief.

Just say "It's for work."

People will nod and understand because work, you see, is for grownups.

People understand that work is an awful thing, and that you probably *have* to be doing whatever you're doing right now. If you're working, you must be doing something important (probably with spreadsheets) because getting together a report for some random executive is definitely more important than fulfilling part of your life's passion.

If you're "working," you *can't* be wasting time because no time has ever been wasted at work. That's for sure.

At the end of your transition, people will marvel at your art. They'll wonder how you found the time or talent to do such a thing. They'll wish they had the ability to do what you do.

But until then, just tell them you're working.

LEARN EVERYTHING

What does the Holocaust have to do with ice cream?

I don't know, but you might.

Look, the Creative makes connections other people don't. She draws lines where they didn't exist before and erase ones that do.

There's a reason people are going nuts about Grey Malin's rainbow colored sheep - it's because he took two things that had nothing to do with each other (bland livestock and the neon colors accompanying most modern design) and mixed them together.

The way to stand out is to look beyond the ordinary. The way to excel is to *combine existing* things nobody has ever seen before. I'm someone who believes there is nothing truly original. There is nothing new under the sun.

Your job is to see the truth in the way you see it.

If you're a writer, that may mean taking things you found from Steven King, adding them with a dab of Ernest Hemingway, and throwing in a bit of Tony Robbins just for good measure.

Creation is always a mix and match approach, not a formula.

People like to pretend that creativity is this massive cerebral process, but more often than not, it's just pin the tail on the neuron. You just ask your brain what's up, and your mental facilities crank out an object, thought, or idea which may or may not be useful.

Creativity is an arcade. Your brain is the crane game.

And learning everything increases the amount of options in your prize bucket.

Here's the Big Secret...

...Nobody feels like an adult.

Nobody feels like a "great man."

Successful creative people did not become successful because they hit some big, magical break.

Successful creative people became successful because they got up every day and did one thing toward their goals. And then they did the same thing the next day. And then they did the same thing the next day.

A lot of people finish chapter one, but some people don't.

A lot of people finish a whole manuscript, but some people don't.

A lot of people even start querying agents, but some people don't.

For every step you take, you create distance between you and your competition if you're into that sort of thing.

If you aren't, you're just creating distance from the person you are and moving toward the person in your dreams. The world-famous one, the unstoppable one, the one who fulfills her potential.

Emotion and motivation are only some of the equation. The rest of the equation requires motion, only nobody talks about the fact that sometimes you are going to boldly go and sometimes you are going to grouchily stumble.

Getting where you want to be is not a great leap forward. It's not a short burst for a moment. It's not a sprint.

It's waking up and taking another step forward,

and another step forward,

and another step forward.

DISCIPLINE

On its best days, creativity is a romp in the park. on its worst, a grueling workout.
(Headband and sweats are optional in either case)

Guess who gives you permission to create?

It's very quiet at my house right now.

At 7:49 a.m. on a Saturday, everyone is still sleeping.

This is actually pretty late for me. Usually it's 5:49 a.m. on a weekday.

No, I don't have children, but I do have a full-time job, 5 cats in the house right now (don't get me started), 2 parents (and 3 parents-in-law) which I like to see now and again, a massive extended family which has events all the time, and I also serve on the board of a local professional networking organization.

So I get up early in the morning.

No, not every morning. Some mornings are reserved for cuddles. People who say they can do the 5 A.M. thing every single day are aliens or lying or their wives aren't as pretty as mine.

I don't know how busy you are. If you have kids, I'm guessing your schedule for the day is more stuffed than my stomach after taco night. I don't know what your job demands of you right now. I don't know how many commitments you've taken on.

But I do know this:

Nobody else cares if you have time to create or not.

It doesn't have to be the morning. It can be 1:49 A.M. It can be 12:49 on your lunch break, crouched in the stairwell with your laptop and trying not to get Doritos on your keyboard. It can be with a voice recorder during your commute.

You will never have the time to do your life's work unless you make it a priority. The universe will never allow you to create until you prove you are willing.

Every single creative struggles with discipline.

I promise you, every artist from Steven King to Boz Lurman to J.K. Rowling to you will have trouble getting started some days. If you've struggled with creating a habit, you're in good company.

There is an incredible book called *The War of Art* written by Steven Pressfield which I consider must-read material for all budding Creatives. Until you read that (or even if you've already read it) here are some tricks that have worked for me, and might work for you too:

1. Do your thing first
Your schedule shows your priorities. Period.

Mornings are great, of course, but remember, we Creatives don't worship morning like the other gurus out there. If you stay up 'til 3 and wake up at noon, do your work at noon. I personally write most mornings before I even brush my teeth because I get started before my lazy self tells me not to.

2. Do your thing every day

Professional athletes have practice every day. Professional knowledge workers sit at a desk every day. Professional Creatives honor the process every day.

One theory I like is the "No More Zero Days" mindset. If you have written one sentence, even one word, you can call that day a success. Just as long as it isn't zero. When you start your thing every day, it gets hard to not do it. Case in point - I'm writing these particular words in an airport.

3. Do your thing with a timer

Even 15 minutes at a time is awesome. The countdown seems to activate an urgency, which isn't as bad as it sounds. Setting a timer both reminds you how fast time passes AND how much you can get done in a short amount of time.

4. Do your thing for someone else's good

My life changed whenever I got married. All of a sudden I had this other person I wanted to support and love and keep company. Building a career in writing seemed like a great way to provide while fulfilling my unspoken obligation of being happy.

Doing things only for yourself has a limit – in both the literal and the spiritual sense.

5. Split your thing up into smaller things

The temptation for the new Creative is to try and write a whole novel in a week. When he realizes it's going to take longer than that, he gets frustrated and gives up.

Give yourself something meaningful to accomplish (I am going to paint 45 minutes today. I am going to write 750 words today) and then go from there.

Some is always better than none.

6. Reward yourself for doing your thing

Much like the monkey in the cage who does sign language for grapes, we humans also love to be rewarded for our labor. Whenever you do check that box for the day, make sure to treat yourself.

This is simply a form of positive feedback (albeit a crude one). Want to know why people enjoy their jobs for 20 years? They've created an *infinite loop* of positive feedback. They don't need a reward because the work *is* the reward.

7. Actually like the thing you are doing

One of the biggest reasons people procrastinate or flat-out avoid what they are trying to do is because they don't actually want to do that thing in the first place.

Please don't be those people.

If becoming an artist is something you know you want to do or be, let your love for the craft pull you through. Otherwise QUIT IT.

Life is too short to operate outside your calling.

8. Find a new tool to make your thing more fun
I hated drawing. Until I discovered Adobe Illustrator. For me, the challenge of learning a new program or idea or craft is often enough in itself to keep me coming back to the desk.

9. Plug your thing into your core driver
Your core driver is an emotion or feeling which gets you up in the morning. It picks you up when you are down, keeps you running when you are tired, and spurs you to action when you are lazy.

One of mine is competition, which is why the timer thing works so well. But I am constantly reminding myself that by showing up each day, by creating more work, I am going to beat 97% of the people who are sitting at home, talking about what they could do if they had the time.

. . .

Ooh, a list of nine. Sorry OCD readers.

Remember, when it comes to discipline, it's not about *will* you struggle, *what you will do* once the struggle begins?

Priorities

Here is a list of things I'm tempted to do instead of writing this passage:

1. Improve my website
2. Schedule some blog posts
3. Check on some freelance work
4. Develop business ideas I have for a place down the street
5. Go back to bed and sleep/cuddle
6. Catch up on my Facebook notifications (Because that's important)
7. Catch up on email (because that is important and business-like)
8. Read
9. Clean up (my office is a wreck)
10. Think about things to write about (the trickiest of temptations)

Most of those items *seem* productive. Most of them *seem* like good ways to spend my time.

What we have here is a situation of priorities.

Often when you are a Creative hustling to make a name for herself, you will have to make difficult decisions about how to spend your free time. Let me provide a guide for these priorities:

Priority #1: Creating new art

Priority #2: Everything else

"Before my 'real' job?"

No. To be a sustained Creative, income is more than a little helpful. Do not flush away your primary source of bill-paying to keep a streak alive.

Remember, I said "*FREE time.*" If you only have twenty minutes of free time after work and before dinner, attack those minutes and make new stuff.

"What about my family?"

Do not leave your children to starve on the table because you need to check the box for that day. I'm not a parent, but that doesn't seem like the best way to go about things. Give some attention to your spouse. "The Dream" is not the dream if you alienate those closest to you.

"But isn't an online presence more important?"

No. A Creative creates. Period. The difference between someone who wants to paint for a living and

THE CREATIVE'S CURSE

one who wants to paint for a hobby is one of them *actually* paints every day.

"What if I'm in a place where I can't do my art?"

Focus on what you *can* do - if you can't paint/draw, can you doodle on a napkin? If you can't write, can you jot down a note in your phone?

Sometimes you have to get creative to get creative. Everything counts, even drawing in the sand.

"What if I'm on vacation?"

That's really up to you. I've done it both ways with mixed results. These days, vacation implies that I'm completely diving into family. I go all-in at work so I can go all in during vacation as well.

However, if I feel like getting up 20 minutes earlier than everyone to write, I do. If I have a big idea, I'm certainly not going to ignore it.

Again, your call on the balance.

Coming up with ideas is not the priority.

Building a portfolio is not the priority.

Growing your social media following is not the priority.

Making your art is the priority.

Will all those other things have to be done? Of course! You know as well as I do that people who leverage social media (even if they are average artists) can make a big splash in the world.

But for you, Creative, the art must come first because *you must love the work.*

I imagine that if you're reading this book, you have some vague daydream about being able to paint/design/write/sing full-time. Keep in mind that "full-time" means every day. If you don't have the discipline to Create every day when you're doing it for free, you won't have the discipline to do it for money. Your blue-sky imaginary career won't be as fun when you obtain it (just like literally everything else in the world).

You must love the work.

You must *do* the work every day.

End of story.

Discipline Tool #1 – The Free Time Checklist

I didn't want to hate my job.

I really didn't. I mean, it paid the bills. It provided for my family. My boss was incredible.

But I was starting to despise it.

After being in a college environment where I had gobs of time to pursue writing, I was now in a place where 40 hours of my week (minimum) were already spoken for.

I got frustrated.

Then I couldn't write.

Then I got furious.

Why couldn't I make any progress? Where did all my time go? I had all these dreams and goals to make it as a writer, but instead, the words wasted away on my hard drive, unread by anyone.

Been there before?

If you've ever felt like you don't have enough time to create, let's make a change. This is the tool that got me creating again, and more importantly, it got me moving in the right direction.

Along the way, I started a website, built a great Snapchat fam (hey guys), amassed quite a following on Medium (5,000 at time of writing), and made 3 extra guides to run alongside my blog.

Oh, and fyi, I didn't have any sag in my full-time gig. In fact, I increased my salary there… almost $30K.

It's called the Free Time Checklist.

Note — Read that again, only this time sing the Hallelujah chorus. It's better that way

Here's how it works:

Step 1: Define how much "free time" you actually have

Lie to yourself here, and the whole thing falls apart. If you are a single mother with three kids, don't expect 40 more hours to bounce out of nowhere. Be realistic.

I quickly realized I could only expect 10 hours of free time during the week. That's not a lot. But it was all I had.

Take a sheet of paper and lay it out in landscape mode (wider than tall). Be honest with yourself and write that magic number at the bottom right of your page.

BE HONEST.

Okay you got it? Let's move on…

Step 2: Identify all the different things you want to do

In every side hustle, there are other objectives than "just do the thing."

I knew being a writer with influence would take more than just hammering out sentences and asking my mommy how good I was. It was important, but not the only thing.

Couple of things to note here:

At this point I was only posting *once* a week. This seems absurd in a world where everyone has information coming out their eyeballs and have to be in your face ALL THE TIME. Remember, consistency is better than frequency.

This step forces you to get 100% clear about what you're doing and why you're doing it. If an item is less impactful than the rest of the items, kick it off the list.

Step 3: Order the list from most to least important

That's pretty much all that's needed to be said for this step.

Step 4: Estimate how much time you want to spend with each item

Now we're starting to get into real numbers.

Again, be honest. Don't say it's only going to take you 30 minutes to paint something if it takes you 27 just to set up. If it's important to you, you can find the time.

In fact, it's probably a good idea to over-estimate time. Things rarely go as smoothly as you think they will.

Step 5: CHOP

If you're adding up all the minutes and they don't fit the number you put at the top of the page, CUT THEM OUT! Remember, they are the least important things on your list. Trust your instincts.

In my step 5, I had to sacrifice "Building a Website" in place of "Connecting with Others." So I was now planning to be **a blogger without a website**. How was I going to do that?

Didn't matter. What good was a site if I didn't have anything to put on it?

I used Medium as my home and stuck to the plan. You notice "searching for other people to connect with" is pretty high on the list. After a few months doing that,

I struck up a friendship with a blogger who was starting a design service.

A few months later, he built me a site for free.

FOR FREE.

Funny how the world works, isn't it?

Step 6: Go Time

Whenever you get a free moment, GO ALL-IN on your first unchecked item!

You no longer have any excuses. You know what it takes.

Just do it.

Step 7 to ∞: Assess and Re-write

When you do something a lot, you generally get better at it. After a month of working this plan, you may find you're getting through things much faster.

Each week you execute, make sure to note how much time it actually takes you to complete the task. This helps with the honesty AND helps you clarify which things you actually care about.

This tool works whether you have 10 hours or 10 minutes or days of free time. It starts with finding your spare time. And it ends with taking control of it.

Discipline Tool #2 – Micro Journaling

As a writer, I've heard all the arguments for journaling.

It's *reflective*. You *learn* about yourself. It keeps your life in *perspective*.

Blah blah blah.

It wasn't doing it for me.

Whenever I write, I want it to be moving toward something. Even if I know I'll chop a lot in the editing process, it at least feels like progress.

Journaling never felt like progress. I couldn't do it consistently, and if I had to write one more feeling about myself, I would have thrown up.

If you've gone through a similar experience, I suggest something I call "Micro Journaling." It takes a lot less time and effort and still gives me the mental boost I need to get started.

This, far and away, is the number one thing I've done to improve my focus throughout the day.

Here's how it works:

Step 1: Write the date.

For a while, this was the only type of "journaling" I could muster. I literally wrote pages full of nothing but dates like a crazy person.

Recording the day is very important to me. A while back, I went through some awful stuff where I neither knew nor cared what day it was. They were all passing by in one bland, homogeneous mess.

Do not skip this step. By listing every day out, you remind yourself you are alive, you are being intentional, and you acknowledge you will never get another chance to live this day.

Step 2: Make a list of 10(ish) things

Lists make terrible news articles, but great morning brain stretches.

You can either start with a category in mind – "*10 reasons I love my job*" – or you can start by writing down a statement you've been thinking about – "*College is too safe*" – and try and come up with reasons that complement that.

The "college is too safe" statement didn't end up as a category, but a part of a list that was eventually titled

"Reasons people stay in school too long," which will make a good article.

If you're worried about what to write, here's the fun part: *It doesn't really matter* what the list is made of. The whole point, really, of any intellectual morning routine is to make your brain go "hmmm." When the brain goes "hmmm," you move from instinct to higher level thinking.

This is why I suggest writing "10*ish*" items. Do whatever it takes to get to your "hmmm" moment. If you list 10 colors, and you didn't once have to try and remember one, the activity is a worthless. However, if you're me, and can only think about 4 colors at any given moment, this would be a challenge. If your prompt happens to be "Things that could improve the American political system," you might hit the "hmmm" right away.

I wouldn't know. I am much too scared of this topic to try.

It worth noting I don't always think of good ideas in the morning. But I *always* think of more ideas throughout the day after doing this practice.

Step 3: Write one thing you are grateful for

Again, what you're going for is the maximum effect with the minimum amount of time. I don't want you to think about it, I just want to you write the first thing that comes to mind.

I've written "Kate" on several of mine. You can also find such loquacious excerpts as "roof" and "food."

Gratitude is critical. If you can't be thankful for something you already have, you will not be thankful for anything else you achieve that day.

Step 4: Close the book and get back to your life

That's seriously it. The whole process takes anywhere from 3 to 10 minutes, depending on how many things you actually end up writing and how big your "hmmm" is.

I've tried a lot of different elements in my morning routine over the last couple of years, and this is easily my favorite.

For a picture of my Micro Journaling page (and a list of 31 prompts), head over to:
www.toddbrison.com/microjournaling.

One Question

If I were to speak to you today, I would ask this:

> *"What one thing have you done today to move toward your dreams?"*

For me, it's pretty simple. I want to be a writer. Doing a post a week on Medium is simply a step in the road. It's one step.

I want to write a book. Writing these words right now is the step that comes before that.

I don't have lots of followers on Medium because I wrote one great post. I have lots of followers on Medium because I wrote a lot of terrible things nobody cared about and then kept writing anyway.

Every success is just a series of steps. *That's the beauty of it.* Steve Jobs didn't build Apple in one day. He woke up and tinkered with a machine in his garage. He did this every day.

He was obsessed with his vision.

So he simply got up every day and walked toward it.

THE CREATIVE'S CURSE

Successful people don't get successful by leaps and bounds. They get there by putting one foot in front of the other 100,000 times.

What about you?

Are you waiting for an overnight success kind of thing to happen? Are you posting on Instagram only every so often, hoping one of your pictures will get popular and you'll just magically be offered fame and money?

Or are you posting all the time, figuring out how to take better pictures, figuring out what people like to look at, and tackling the world one pixel at a time?

The sad news about being successful is that more often than not, it's boring.

The better news about being successful is that it comes to those who take one boring step today.

Then do it again tomorrow.

And again the next day.

And again forever.

2 Ways to March Your Way Into Recognition

When Tim Ferriss posts something, people flock in droves to read it.

When Gary Vaynerchuk posts a new video, the internet explodes.

When Grey Malin releases a new series of photos featuring rainbow-colored sheep, everyone flings money at him.

They act, people react. No extra effort needed.

But what about those of us still fighting the tide of obscurity? What about those of us who are juggling a family and a full-time job just trying to dig out a couple hours out of the week to create? We'd love to have the luxury of those artists.

The truth is, you may never have the extra time to create. And even if you did, it's likely you would get just as much done. That being said though, there are two things you can do to get attention, even if you don't have the same buzz as the big dogs (yet).

1. Be Consistent

It's no secret that I have commitment issues when it comes to work. Before this year, I never wrote regularly because that felt like work. That which got too familiar became a cage.

So instead, I committed to something small - one post a week on Medium. Just one.

Every Tuesday I would post. Every single Tuesday for 5 months I'd write something and nobody would read it (other than my parents). For those first 20 or so posts, I didn't get much recognition. Nobody cared.

Then, in the 6th month, something started to change. I wrote a post that got a fairly decent amount of traffic and folks started to come in waves. Some would come to my page and then read everything I'd ever published.

A funny thing happens when you get consistent: By the time the world realizes what you're doing, **they think you belong there**. In the first 5 months, I had less than 200 followers. In the next month and a half, I got to almost 2,000. Now Medium is recommending me to new users simply because I write there a lot.

It's not a fluke. I do the same thing with my Motivation Monday series on Snapchat (add me:

+toddbr). It takes 30 minutes with my early-morning coffee. First nobody cared. Now they won't let me stop.

You don't have to post 7 days a week in order to stay relevant. You really don't. We get fooled into thinking the only way we are allowed to write or paint or be creative is to do it full-time.

It's a lie.

The only time you have to write is from 6 -7 a.m. on a Thursday morning? Awesome. Write then.

The only paints you have are blue and the toddler just went down for a nap? Cool. Try something monochromatic.

The only time you have access to a studio is once a month? Fine. Work out lyrics during your commute.

Find your rhythm. Do what you can. Refuse to feel guilty about the rest.

2. Use Momentum

You've heard the phrase "an object in motion tends to stay in motion?"

It applies to creativity too.

One dark and stormy November 31st many years ago, I was trying to hit a NaNoWriMo (National Novel

THE CREATIVE'S CURSE

Writing Month) deadline. I had 3 hours to write just over 4,500 words. It was impossible. I didn't even know what was going to happen next in the story. No clue how it was going to turn out.

Do you know what I did?

I started.

I started with the hope that the pieces would fall into place. I wrote one sentence and then another and then another. After a while, I couldn't stop. My bladder ached and my stomach growled, but I was going to *make* it.

Creativity doesn't always come. The ideas don't always flow freely. But when they do, **for God's sake, ride the wave.** Ride it as long as you can. You know that hour on Thursday morning you have set aside to write? On the days you finish early, *don't finish early*. Just keep going.

Some days, heck, some *weeks* I have absolutely no time to write. But every time I step on a plane, you can bet I'll crank out at least 2,500 words.

Starting is hard. Staying is easy.

Once you start being consistent, it's easier to create things. Once it's easier to create things, you can create more of them in less time.

Consistency and momentum are small things that create a big impact.

It's not sexy to say "do this for 2 years and *then* people will care."

But sometimes that's what it takes.

Dear Person Stifling Creativity at Your Job

What if I told you creativity is bigger than the box you put it in?

What if I told you creativity is more than your drawing, your writing, or your imagination?

See, a lot of people get hung up and claim they can't be creative at work because they don't work in marketing. They aren't in customer service. They don't have the power to do something new.

And they are all wrong.

Creativity, in its purest sense, is connecting dots which weren't before. It's bringing a new mindset, a new point of view, a new idea to something old.

Rarely is creativity a birthing of something completely new and original. More often, it's just improving (or reworking) what already exists.

If that's the case, you can be creative in everything.

Do you have a new solution for how you process data? Awesome, spit it out.

Do you think the slide desks should be organized differently? Excellent, do it.

Show me a person who says they can't be creative at work but doodles on every piece of paper they find, and I'll show you a liar.

To be a Creative is to be creative in *all* things.

Don't leave your talent on the living room couch.

This is the Middle of the Book

I've reached the point where I'm realizing just how much work there is left to do on this book.

I'm reading passages I wrote a week ago and they are terrible.

I'm losing sight of the message I wanted to send in the first place.

I'm tempted to quit and move on to something else (it's easy. I've done that plenty.)

This is all normal.

If you are a Creative, at some point, you will absolutely hate what you've made. It is usually accompanied by a cooing voice in the back of your head telling you to just jump ship.

Remember this - anything you do must be redone. Painters don't try and work around their first few brush strokes, *they go over them.* The first coat is just a foundation.

The easy way out is to give it up and move on to something else. Plenty of people have done just that. These are people you will never hear about.

I bet you have stories which were never finished. I bet you have ideas you've never written down. I bet you have photographs you've never shown anyone.

The middle is the hardest part. I haven't run a marathon, but I'm told miles 13-15 are the worst. (I think I understand that analogy though because I always have trouble finding the mental energy to get past World 4 of Super Mario 3.)

The middle is the hardest part because a Creative is, by nature, obsessed with ideas. They are fueled by them. Ideas are the whole reason you started. Once the idea becomes familiar it is much less attractive.

Canoe trips are fun at first, but when you can't see the finish line and you can't see where you pushed off from and you've run out of sandwiches and beer, they aren't really that much fun anymore.

But you still have to finish. A Creative cannot live on ideas alone. She needs the discipline to see ideas through because someone needs to hear what she is saying. Someone needs to hear what *you* have to say, too.

Without discipline, you may as well have never thought of the idea in the first place. It's time to finish.

BLINK

Blink.

The cursor mocks you.

Blink. Blink.

You've been staring at this blank page for ten minutes wondering how to start.

Blink. Blink. Blink.

This has never been a problem before. You've written plenty of times. Just the other day you had a great idea! Now it won't come back.

Blink. Blink. Blink. Blink.

The first thing you should know is that writer's block is NOT a creative problem. No matter how many days you've written in a row, there is always more to write. Ideas are only the combination of things which already exist. Given that definition, new ideas are infinite.

The second thing you should know is that generally, you can get started simply by starting.

The third thing you should know is that your output on any given day does not ostracize you from being a Creative.

Have you accepted those three things? Good. Let's try and diagnose the problem further. Here are 6 possibilities.

1. You are afraid.
I haven't tested every human being in the planet, but my guess is that Creatives are among the MOST fearful. This is because back in early humanity, it was difficult to fend off a lion with a paintbrush.

2. You think other Creatives are way better than you.
Remember - you only see the end product of other authors' work. Odds are the first draft is worse than you could imagine.

3. You are tired.
Give yourself some grace. Humans need to inhale in order to exhale. Creatives need to experience in order to give. Creatives cannot produce 24-7. The quality of our *input* is just as important as the quality of our *output*. Take it easy already.

4. You don't have any ideas.
News flash - ideas don't come from looking at a screen. Ideation and creation are separate. If you're expecting

yourself to come up with ideas WHILE writing them, you're going to have a tough time. Flip back to the "Where Do Ideas Come From" section if you need a reminder.

5. You are trying to write about something you don't care about.
Why?

6. You have no self-discipline.
Let me be the tough guy for a second - any dream, wish, hope, or goal you have for this life demands some attention and effort on your part. The good news is that people aren't born with self-discipline. Most of them just trick themselves into it.

That cursor is probably still blinking while you're reading this book.

It might be time to go stop it.

Excuses

Stop me if you've heard any of these before:

"I'm working on a novel."

Oh really? for the last three years? How's that going?

"I just haven't had any inspiration lately."

Inspiration comes those who are willing to drag it out of the cave and beg for answers.

"I'm not in the mood."

Your boss wouldn't accept that answer. Don't accept it from yourself either.

"I've written everything I can possibly write."

HA!

"I'm tired."

Take a 10 second nap and then draw whatever you wake up thinking about.

If you are waiting for the big idea, the one that changes your life and finally gets people to take you seriously as a creator, it's behind walls of work, hours of struggle, and mountains of effort.Overnight success does not exist.

The Ultimate Guide to Beating Creator's Block

Beating Creator's Block Step 1: Figure Out Why Your Block is (Really) Happening

Here's something people don't ask me now, but when I'm king of the Internet they will:

"Todd! I have writer's block. How do I get out of it?"

And this will be my answer:

"Figure out what you are afraid of."

Let me explain:

I read one time on the Internet that writer's block is a myth, which is something I don't really believe. Writer's block is a real thing, but the *name* is misleading.

Back when I was in college, I wrote a piece for the school newspaper that got very popular (well, as popular as school newspaper articles get).

After that week of floating on high-fives and thumbs-ups, I proceeded to write absolutely nothing for the next several months. I was still on staff for the paper. I was actually the editor for the sports section. But I wrote zero.

It was my longest drought since I started writing.

The big gap between articles had nothing to do with a lack of ideas (I still had plenty) or a lack of talent (I knew I could write).

It come from something else, a characteristic we see in all humans, from clock-puncher to chef to Creative:

Fear.

The name "writer's block" leads us to believe we are facing a creative problem, like the Muse has somehow gone silent.

Reminder: there are an infinite amount of words to be written, topics to explore, dots to connect, and new ideas to probe. There will always be something to create.

If ideas are any part of your job, and you've been coming up dry recently, the first step is to identify what you are afraid of. Here are some things that might be keeping you from your best work (yes, I've been through all of them):

1. Fear of failure

The obvious one. What if your next work isn't as good as the first? What if nobody listens to you ever again? What if this is the peak of your career and you have to scrawl messages on the bathroom wall instead because they shut down your Internet for being the worst writer of all time?

The downward spiral goes pretty far.

The Cure: Create and publish something else as soon as possible. Enjoy the transition back to obscurity.

2. Fear of success

This one is a little trickier. It usually has to do with an underlying belief telling you success as a Creative is something you don't deserve, like you are cheating the world for being good at your work *and* enjoying it.

Let me tell you right now - you deserve it.

The Cure: Make Creation a routine. Maintaining a routine takes work. Work deserves compensation.

3. Fear of alienating your new fans

Nice going on hitting that spike in traffic! You've finally got some new blood in your audience. This next post needs to be a blended article that can be enjoyed from everyone to the 19-year-old biology major to the

67-year-old retiree. And it needs to be funny too. And it needs to touch the hearts of every nationality.

Yeah. Good luck with that.

The Cure: Remember who you're writing for. It's not the thousands of people who read that one article. It's the tens of people who read everything you've ever written.

4. Fear of new expectations

This is sort of like fear of success but with one minor twist - maybe you don't have time to be a professional Creative.

Another immediate pressure that comes with success is "you should write more." People will ask questions and expect answers. Don't change your rhythm (aka post 7 times a week instead of your usual 2) just because you think someone wants you to.

Remember, *you will fear a cage the most*. Don't allow Creativity itself to become that cage.

The Cure: Stick to your game plan. The world is noisy, and when your audience grows, you will feel pressure to just feed the animals. Don't give in. Just keep doing what you do best.

5. Fear of Chumbawamba-ism

"I get knocked down, but I get up again. You're never gonna keep me down!"

Ah, yes, the infamous one-hit wonders. If you are even the slightest bit like me, your first success as a Creative will send you reeling down a train of thought that reminds you of every one-hit wonder that ever lived.

You will start to feel perhaps it's your fate to join them. Your one big contribution to the world is now over and you should meet up with these Chumbawumba fellows and have coffee or something. You can talk about your 15 minutes of fame over an iced frappy-latte thing. (Sorry, I'm not in Starbucks that much)

You don't get to decide what the masses care about. You only need to create more stuff.

The Cure: Remind yourself there is only one choice you control: Whether you keep creating or whether you quit.

Writer's Block is a real thing. Creatives really do go through ruts. It *always* starts with fear.

Now when it comes knocking, you'll be able to call it what it is, laugh in its face, and get back to work.

Beating Creator's Block Step 2: Build Creative Triggers

Before Steven Pressfield starts his work, he pours a cup of coffee, puts on his lucky work boots, ties his lucky laces, sits in the same chair every day, points his lucky toy cannon toward himself for ideas, says a prayer, and *then* dives into his writing.

His pre-work routine (which includes much more than listed here) takes him until about 10:30 A.M. to complete.

Does that sound a little crazy? You bet.

Is it successful? Well, he wrote *The Legend of Bagger Vance*, which was turned into a movie that made millions. So you tell me.

It's fine if you aren't into rubbing acorns or turning in circles before you create, but the brain is nothing if not responsive to familiar stimuli.

Creating a creative trigger for yourself will allow you to take the same power which makes you happy when you hear a certain song and apply it to your work.

When you start this practice, do your best to use triggers which don't already carry a particular memory or emotion. You can certainly overwrite them, but it'll take more time.

Being intentional about what you pair your work with can turn you into a creative machine, coming up with ideas at the drop of the hat, and doing more work faster.

Use the most primitive parts of the human condition - the senses. Different people respond better or worse to different senses, but here's an example of how you can use each one.

Try each of these. You probably don't know what sense you respond most strongly to.

Remember: Bring these triggers into your office, your desk, your studio, or whatever place you create most often.

Smell

Smells in particular have a very powerful effect on the brain. Think about the last time you walked into a foul, dank gas station bathroom. My guess is you couldn't think about much else.

No matter what the odor, smells ground you in the exact moment. Using them whenever you create can send you into "flow" easier (more on flow later).

Experiment with these:

- Tea or coffee (I actually recommend against coffee because it's usually already coupled to so many other memories. A particular flavor of tea is best)
- Candles
- Air fresheners or plugins
- An open window (inconsistent, but can be effective)

Sight

We're not looking for the kind of images on your desk which take your breath away. Those are much too distracting. We're looking for something small: not glamorous, but meaningful. Remember the goal here - you're looking for a subtle, familiar things

Experiment with these:

- An inspirational quote on a post-it
- The same room every time
- Nonsense words at the top on your otherwise empty document (a page with random words like "foo bar zing bang" at the beginning is easier to work with than an empty one)

- Clutter-free work spaces

There's a very cool caveat about sight triggers - *the work itself* can become a trigger. Think about how much easier it is to work once there's already something on the canvas.

Touch

This trigger isn't necessarily "touching" with your hands or finger, but it's more like "feeling"

Many great thinkers walked around twiddling something in their hands, but if your work isn't hands-free, you'll have to come up with some other options.

Experiment with these:

- Spend some time with the object of your creation before you even start (brush, pen, phone, whatever)
- Sit in the same chair (remember, it's "feeling," not touching)
- Drape a blanket around your shoulders
- Use a space heater to warm your fingers

For me, the feeling of my fingers flying across the keyboard combined with the words appearing across the screen is one of my most powerful triggers. It inspires me to keep writing, which becomes a nearly infinitely loop (which explains my racing to the bathroom after 5 hours of constant immersion).

Sound

If you have a computer, this is probably the easiest trigger to manipulate.

iTunes can work, but most people have playlists that are too distracting. The ideal music disappears into the background.

I recommend going to SoundCloud and putting together a quick group of songs (preferably classical or otherwise non-lyrical). Build something about an hour long for starters, as it's difficult to work continuously with anything longer.

Only add music with words if you have already heard them hundreds of times. You want the volume to be high enough where you can hear it, but just barely. If you're straining to listen, it's too soft. If you're singing along, it's too loud.

I don't have a list of options below because honestly, music is the best sound trigger I can imagine. Just find what works for you.

Taste

This one can be trickier because obviously it's difficult find flow with a face full of mashed potatoes.

The key here is to find something which takes minimal effort or time to ingest, but doesn't get in your way

Try these:

- Wine (I recommend only one glass. The whole "write drunk, edit sober thing" has never worked for me)
- Tea or Coffee (again)
- Gum (remember, a specific kind)
- The green swizzle stick thing from your Starbucks cup (chewing plastic is a bad habit, but it worked for me)

The goal with all of these is to take out the variables. The fewer variables you have in any given creative session, the easier it is to focus on the thing that actually matters:

Your work.

Beating Creator's Block Step 3: Finding Flow at the Drop of a Hat

The room melts away, the world fades to black, and you can't focus on anything else but the task in front of you.

You are completely consumed by the work. It doesn't matter, now if you've left the oven on or if you're having money trouble.

The only thing that matters is the flourish of brush on a page, the choice of exactly the right word, or the snap of a perfect photo right before the subject moves.

Welcome, my friends, to flow.

"Flow" is a concept coined by Mihály Csíkszentmihályi, in the early 80s. This researcher wanted to know exactly how to create an "optimal experience" under any conditions. (p.s. don't read the book unless you are prepared to go to war. It's horribly dull and long and after these concepts I'm about to introduce, doesn't have much to say except case study after case study.)

Some of the greatest work of all time comes from flow. Think of the athlete who describes "being in the zone" and not remembering much of what went on in the game.

To give you a primitive definition, flow is simply **the balance between anxiety and boredom.** It's walking the fine line where your task is challenging and you have the skills to complete it. If your skills aren't enough to take on the challenge, your *incompetence* makes you *anxious*. If your skills are far beyond the challenge at hand, your *over-qualification* makes you *bored*.

Get it?

Csíkszentmihályi points out the conditions of flow don't just have to happen naturally, they can be created.

It's simple - the more flow you achieve, the more work you produce.

Let's take a quick look ways to work ourselves into flow:

1. Create a challenge that is not too great for our skills

For most areas of life, this is pretty straightforward. If you are just learning to cook, you probably should start with scrambled eggs, not lamb chop with a balsamic reduction.

New Creatives often get in trouble because we get caught up in a moment and think "I'm going to write a novel!" without realizing the challenge. They get overwhelmed by the challenge at hand because they've never done it before. They don't yet have the skills to sit down, create 50,000 or so words, and then order them into a coherent message.

Instead, a good goal would be to first sit down and write 500 words at a time, then 750, then 1,000. You can (and I have) go for broke and sprint through 5,000 words, but it's not for the untrained.

Here's the good news - there is no finish line for the artist. There will always be new challenges to solve both in the way of technique (improving vocabulary, learning a new brush stroke, figuring out a new technology) and in message (who is this for and how can I best communicate it to them).

2. Define clearly the goals and subgoals

During the month of November, thousands of people set out on a goal - to write a novel in 30 days.

THE CREATIVE'S CURSE

NaNoWriMo started out as an idea but exploded in popularity as almost everyone thinks they have a novel in them.

One of the reasons this program excels is because of its very clear goals and subgoals.

Instead of just saying "write a novel in 30 days," writers are given a black-and-white target: 50,000 words. By creating a clear goal, participants know exactly whether or not they have succeeded.

It gets even deeper than that. On the NaNoWriMo website, future authors are also given a daily word count subgoal (about 1800 words). Now they have a clear task for each day, not just the whole month.

Solid goals, not just vague targets, are critical for every flow experience. Don't believe me? Think about how popular American football has become. That game is littered with goals and subgoals:

Goal: Win the game*Subgoals*:

- Score points. You score points by…
- Getting from one end of the field to the other. You get more time to achieve that subgoal by…
- Getting first downs. You get first downs by…
- Gaining 10 yards. You gain 10 yards by…

- Gaining one yard at a time. You gain one yard at a time by…
- Running good plays.

And that's just the offensive side of the ball.

Goals and subgoals make flow effortless. It works in football. It works in creativity.

3. Eliminate distraction

In one of his studies on flow, Csíkszentmihályi, wanted to know just how much brain activity was going on when a person was in flow.

He expected to find a high level of brain function, and that higher levels of consciousness gave the participants a good time.

Makes sense, right?

The results proved him *wrong*.

Instead of high levels of brain activity, the participants in the study who reported the most enjoyable experiences actually had *much less* brain activity than their less-than-pleased counterparts.

The reason? Less distraction.

Remember when we talked about the feeling of the world fading away? That's not a figure of speech. The brain, little by little, is shutting down the parts of your mind which notices other stimuli. In the highest moments of flow, the only parts of the brain active are those devoted to the task at hand - be that writing or swimming or even having a conversation.

Symptoms of this include time passing rapidly, outside noises becoming less noisy (like your wife asking you to wash the dishes), and even tunnel vision - where the person in question doesn't even see the naked woman running next to his computer screen. (True story)

The creative triggers we talked about in the previous section are critical to this process. The less new information for the brain, the better flow is achieved.

We'll get into an advanced lesson on how to eliminate distraction later, but for now, just know it's a big deal.

4. Growth and Continuation of Flow

Let me ask you this - how much time do you spend rehearsing the alphabet these days? My guess is "not much" (unless you are a toddler and have pulled yourself away from Dora the Explorer to read this. Many thanks. Also – mad props). That's because your skills have catapulted above the initial challenge of memorizing all these strange new symbols.

There's a reason 72% of people report being bored at work - their skills outstripped the challenges a 9 to 5 brings. Instead of looking for a new challenge, they instead sink into unrest, even if they may not know why.

This is not an option for Creatives.

Remember – *there is no finish line in art*. The Creative is always doing something new, learning something new, and becoming something new. It's the only way to stay fresh.

The Muse lives within flow. She longs to meet you there.

Go get her.

Beating Creator's Block Step 4: Lies the Brain Tells

If you are a human, you may have noticed from time to time, the brain actually tries to *stop* you from doing what you love most.

It's not its fault. That part is still left over from the survival of the fittest days. Those little electronic pulses up in your skull think you are safe right now. Which is great! And a problem.

Because you have to make art consistently. Consistent art production means a life change. The brain doesn't like life changes, so it will feed you lies to keep you from risk.

Recognize these lies for what they are, kick them to the curb, and then move on.

#1

"Everything will be fine if you don't do this, you know."

Yeah, it will, actually. You will be fine if you stay the way you are forever. You will be fine if you never hit any of your big goals or dreams.

You will be fine if you never write that book.

Lots of people do fine.

But it's not for you.

#2

"This is not THAT important"

Yes it is. You becoming the version of yourself you've only dreamed about up to this point is critical.

Reminder - *You* define what is "important." Don't let the lizard brain or your girlfriend or society or your mother try and talk you out of it.

Breathe in what you want. Visualize it coming to life. Imagine how you will feel when you finally write that last word, take that perfect snapshot, or sell that first painting.

Are you there? Can you feel the emotions? Do you taste the moment?

It is not only important you become who you mean to. It is imperative.

#3

"What good would it do to finish this? Nobody cares about you"

That's probably true. Nobody cares about anyone else for the most part. They care about themselves.

THE CREATIVE'S CURSE

Here's an interesting trick—pretend you're invisible. Seriously. Because to 99.999% of the world, you probably are.

The realization that most people don't care about your work might just be the most freeing thing that ever happens to you.

#4

"But we're safe with what we have! Best not do anything to jeopardize that."

It's the job of your brain to protect you. But seeing as there aren't a whole lot of wild hippogriffs running around these days, let's face it—we're all pretty safe.

Lacking a proper stimulus, the mind then sets about worry for our careers. Which is a fair fear. At the rate that technology is replacing us, no job is safe.

That's okay, though. Comfort is overrated.

Change is coming. You can either ride the wave or be dragged to death.

#5

"You've done enough"

What is "enough" anyway? Is it less than what you thought it was? Less than what you are capable of? Is it a dollar sign?

How can you have done "enough" if you are still breathing? What's the alternative? To *stop* doing things?

Do not let fear determine how much is enough. If you have had enough, fine. If you need to call it a day or take a step away or quit for a while, that's cool.

Let me remind you, though, it's generally the things we *don't* do which are a source of regret.

#6

"Wait, didn't [fill in name of role model] already do this?"

It's possible. Maybe even probable. There's a lot of stuff out there.

All I know is that your thing is different. If you bring in your story, your perspective, your mindset into a new project, nobody will have ever done anything exactly like it.

It's like Bruce Lee said: "Absorb what is useful. Discard what is not. Add what is uniquely your own."

#7

"OH GOD THIS IS TERRIBLE. THIS WHOLE PROJECT/BOOK/SONG IS TERRIBLE. I AM TERRIBLE."

Ooh, I love this one! If you're getting this one, it means you're so close. So very very very very close.

When you start approaching a significant change — the launch of a book, the release of a website, the first day of a new job — your brain will likely panic.

Swallow the fight-or-flight drama, take the last few steps, and do what you're meant to do.

It's time.

The Answer is No

To late-night drinks.
To a 90-minute lunch in the middle of the day.
To water cooler gossip.
To the 2 hours of small talk on the plane.
To the party after the party.
To the meeting you don't have to be in.

The answer is no.

If you want to create things that matter, things that really matter, you'll have to get used to saying this.

This isn't about being an aloof artist (which you can't afford to be). This isn't about being the entrepreneur who checks out from all the relationships you have (which is suicide). This is about rejecting those who want your physical presence in order to pour into those who need your emotional presence.

Because nobody is going to give you time to create.

Nobody is going to say "George, I heard you're trying to make it as a photographer! Why don't you just take some time between 1 and 3 to leave your desk, go outside, and get some great shots for your portfolio."

Not in this world.

Instead, you'll have to cut out some of the things you're currently saying yes to. This doesn't mean you are a jerk. This means you are conscious about how few minutes there are on this planet. This means you are willing to sacrifice some *short-term pleasure* for *long-term impact*.

My coworkers know I don't go out that often. I came in politely declining nearly everything. Now, when I do go out, it's a lot more fun (for me and for them).

Stop complaining about how much of your time is already spoken for and start figuring out a way to get it back.

It doesn't have to be morning, but I'm sure you've got some minutes there.
It doesn't have to be lunch, but I'm sure you can sneak away for a bit then.
It doesn't have to be at midnight, but you can sure make progress when everyone else is sleeping.

Your hours of quiet are not going to appear suddenly, you have to fight for them. Win the Muse. Gain her respect.

And then speak into the silence.

The Weird and Wonderful Characteristic Most People Don't Have

"I don't know, I'm just not seeing any traction."

"How long have you been at it?"

"I've written a post every day for 3 weeks now!"

This conversation happens way too often.

Maybe you've even had it yourself. (I have)

Maybe you thought, like so many of us, that you deserve to be successful already.

Maybe you wonder what it really takes to be a successful creative person.

There's one thing everybody needs, but few have. It's a big key to running the marathon of life without wanting to stick your head in the oven:

Patience.

It doesn't come easily to most (myself included) because we creative types were born to fly.

We were made to run, not walk.

We were meant to sprint, not wait.

We were created to blaze trails, not follow them.

But Life qualifies you. It does it every day. If you aren't willing to keep writing for 6 months when nobody's reading, are you really going to be willing to do it forever?

When I seriously started making a run at being an "online presence" in 2015 (after 1 failed blog, 1 hardly successful one, and a failed business), I knew I couldn't fall into the same trap I did before — trying to do everything at once.

Here's a piece of advice I picked up somewhere. Hopefully it will help you as much as it did me:

Do ONE thing.

If you want to be a photographer, take one picture. One good picture. Then do that for two weeks.

After you've got that down, post one of your pictures. JUST one.

There are no "6 easy steps" to learning patience. I'm not even sure I can tell you how to do it. I can just give you my experience and let you learn from it.

My experience is this:

On January 12, 2015 ALL I DID was record one Monday Motivation for around 30 followers on Snapchat. Maybe 12 of them watched the whole thing. Then I did that for the rest of January.

In February of 2015 I started turning those into articles on Medium. I didn't have a Wordpress site, but still wanted to get my work out there.

I did this for several months, getting better at writing, cranking out Monday Motivation quicker each time. Turning each video into a written article a little faster.

I was doing TWO things. ONLY two things.

I wanted to build a site, but I didn't.

I wanted to publish more, but I didn't.

I wanted to do more, but I didn't.

Four agonizing months later, when I started getting really comfortable with TWO things, I started writing another post a week.

Three things??! Slow down, Todd!

After another two months that felt like an eternity, I got my blog started and wrote two posts a week there and one original piece for Medium each week.

WOAH! FOUR THINGS.

THE CREATIVE'S CURSE

And that's still pretty much where I am. I do four things. Maybe I'll do more one day, but I don't know. Four things is a lot.

Something else strange happens when you are patient. A weird addendum that people don't talk about much because it's hard to explain. In fact, I'm guessing I'll lose a lot of you at this point.

When you keep patient long enough, the world starts playing along.

It's beautiful and wonderful and magical and I don't get it. But it's real. This weird cycle emerges:

Action builds momentum. Momentum builds respect. Respect leads to assistance. Assistance leads to inspiration. Inspiration sparks action.

Here are some things that have happened while I've been patient with four or less things (without much other effort on my part):

- I've had 4 top-20 posts in the world on Medium (2 top-10s).
- I've grown my Snapchat following, connecting with dozens of new people.

- This guy named Matt built me a website FOR FREE.

- One of the editors for LinkedIn asked me to republish one of my pieces in their network.

- A developer approached me about demo-ing his software (don't tell him I'm not super successful and famous).

- My salary at my "real job" grew by about $10K. (Turns out when I don't feel guilty about my side-hustle, I do better at work too).

- And I swear this just happened when I was editing this — someone emailed me on behalf of the New York Observer, asking if they could use my content.

The whole point of me telling you any of that was to tell you this:

Don't be embarrassed to start small.

Start small and grow big. Be faithful with the little things. Love them. Do them well. Do them a lot. Do them in the way only you can do them. Care for them.

And then do another thing.

And then another.

And then another. (maybe)

Rather than spitting out clichés on how every journey starts with a single step, I'll end instead with this question:

If you could skip all the small steps. If you could skip all the climb and the grind and the hustle and the waiting and get what you think you want most…

What on earth would you plan to do for the rest of your life?

DESTINY

There is nothing quite so beautiful and tragic as the professional Creator.

Here's the thing.

Most people, at some point, will try and convince you to take what you've learned and soar. They'll say you should shove away everyone trying to hold you down and TAKE OFF LITTLE BIRD!

There's a problem with that:

Making a living on your own – one that pays all the bills and feeds your wife and kids is very,
very,
very,
difficult.

Throughout history, Creative people have been underpaid. Just because there is more excess in the world than ever before and you read a blog post about making income online that lasts forever does not mean you are entitled or should expect to support your life on your art alone.

It wouldn't be fair for me to ask you to risk everything and go it alone because a) you can learn a lot from other people b) you might not have the business mindset it takes to work alone c) being poor sucks and d) life should not suck.

Here are a few reasons pimping out your art for "The Man" might not be so bad:

1. You get a paycheck

Remember the "being poor sucks" bullet?

2. Companies *need* Creatives

Worse than ever, as it turns out. Computers can replace anything. Anything except ideas.

3. Every Creative needs something to push against

My current boss and I have an understanding - When I create stuff for her, I'm not going to think about what's "corporately accepted." I'm going to include inappropriate jokes and essentially be as wild as I can. That way, when the edits come back and she pulls me in, the project isn't as bad as it would have been.

If I'm afraid to go out of my comfort zone, the work turns into bland snooze-a-thons. That's why I always start wild and assume someone else will reel me back in.

Without an opposing force, Creativity is nearly pointless. If all you do is create what people expect and enjoy, that's not very Creative is it?

4. Paycheck gives you the ability to build something on the side

Again, I DO NOT WANT YOU TO BE A STARVING ARTIST (have I said this enough yet?). Whenever you work for someone, not only do they pay for you to get better, you can take those new skills and sell them to other people.

It's a total racket.

Go on Fiverr. Rebrand a local company. Start a blog. Connect with people in your industry (another thing that's hard to do on without the structure of a 9-5).

Do all those things, but most of all –

Don't jump until you're ready.

The 6-step guide to selling your soul for money

If you decide the independent life isn't for you, you may as well do corporate life right.

There's an interesting conflict which occurs as soon as a creative person steps into a grey, bland corporate office.

He turns into a raging Gorilla-Beast dying to be free.

This beast does his own thing, ignores all advice and criticism, and makes whatever he wants for whomever he wants whenever he wants.

There's an obvious problem here:

Even Gorilla-Beasts need to pay the bills.

That, my friends, is how we end up with the eternal struggle -

Creative vs. Corporate.
Muse vs. Machine.
Breaking Free vs. Buttoning Up.

The truth is, most (almost all) Beasts like yourself will be forced to work for a Corporate Tamer from time to time. And although your art is your soul, you'll have to turn tricks for cash to keep from going hungry.

Here's how to sell your soul without losing your mind:

Step 1 - Give Your Paycheck Some Purpose

Remember the coolest thing about working for a company?

They pay you.

They pay you whether you come in and sit in a chair or you come in and check emails for 8 hours or you come in and actually (wait for it) do your work.

Do not use this money to pile up needless junk you don't need. Use it to build your catapult. The one which will launch you over the walls of the corporate prison. Money gives you leverage. Build enough leverage, and you can pretty much do whatever you want all the time.

The only goal of accepting corporate money is to purchase a key that will free you from the cage, not buy more bars for it.

Step 2 - Go Wild or Go Home

I mentioned this earlier, but I want to remind you again: if you start out boring, your work will always be boring.

Play it safe at first, and people will say - "This looks good," but they don't know how good you could be. They don't know the full potential of the Beast.

Instead, push the envelope early and often. Go a little too far. Publish first, edit later. Give them what they didn't know they were looking for.

For the first few months, let your Gorilla run rampant. Make bold and shocking work.

Warning: this advice will earn you a lot of criticism. Which leads us to step 3.

Step 3 - Take Criticism Like a Champ
"I don't get it."

This sentence will rock you if you're not ready for it. *Your* goal is to express your creativity. *Their* goal is to send a message. So when it's not exactly what they expect, they'll say:

"I don't get it."

Remember the question of doubt we conquered in the Discovery phase? Of *course* they don't get it. If they got it, they would do it themselves. If you were a button-pusher, they wouldn't need you. Computers push all the buttons now.

Whenever your work is picked apart, the Gorilla-Beast will roar in shame and indignation. Stroke him gently and calm down. Every time you tweak your message, you learn a little bit more about what your Tamer wants.

Companies need creators, but they don't need Prima Donnas.

Create. Listen. Adapt. Repeat.

And then move along.

Step 4: Become the Company

If you've been able to control your Beast this far, congratulations! You are starting to earn some trust. People (foolishly) are starting to assume you are a normal human being.

You have earned their trust. This is good.

Once you know where all the lines are, you can bump right up against them. You know what they people want, so give it to them. Give them everything they expect and add a sprinkle of your own flair.

There is no "me" there is only "us." You make your teammates look good. You make your boss look good. You make the company look good.

Become the voice, hands, and face of your company. Become irreplaceable, knowing what clients need before they even ask. Become indispensable. Become the Beast everyone knows and loves.

And then...

Step 5: Leave

Not in a blaze of glory with both middle fingers extended, as the Beast might prefer, but graciously. Leave them happy you ever made it into their lives.

Leaving is a critical piece because when the Beast sits in one place too long and his fire will go out. Don't kid yourself: you are a restless soul. Don't trick yourself into thinking your natural habitat is too dangerous.

No great work comes from safety anyway.

Step 6: Repeat until you can free the Beast

If you took step one to heart, you should be using that cash to build something that matters. If you're not to the point where you can let your soul run wild, take a job that pays more money. Then repeat this process.

No Creative was meant to be put in a cage.

Let's make sure you don't stay in one forever.

THE CREATIVE'S CURSE

THERE WILL BE DAYS YOU DON'T WANT TO GET OUT OF BED.

Days where you will be driven by the voice of the critics alone.

Days where you will design work to appease everyone; and therefore appeal to no one.

Days where you can't handle the weight of a Creative mind.

Days where you hate yourself for writing stupid sentences like that because there are people in the world who have much bigger problems.

Days where you are tired.

Days where you want to quit.

Days where you think to give up.

Days where you want to go back to that person nobody knew.

Days where you would gladly crawl back under your mom's Toy Story comforter if it meant you didn't have to face the world alone.

Days where you just want to be safe.

Days where, no matter how hard you try, you can't even think of a positive way to finish a passage.

How to Be Creative in a Non-Creative Role

There's a name for people who are creative but doesn't possess any artistic skill:

It's "the ideas guy."

The world doesn't need people who come to work and push buttons. Think about it. We're making machines to push all the buttons for us. Taxes, driving, and cooking are all fair tasks for machines in the near future.

By the way, if you *are* a button pusher, it's long past time to start watching your back.

All companies need creative people. Ideas are lifeblood. People and machines can be employed to implement those ideas, but the spark of innovation will always* come from humanity.

I shouldn't say always. It's probably only a matter of time until the robots take over, but humor me for a second, will you?

Creativity gives you the X Factor, the secret sauce at work.

THE CREATIVE'S CURSE

Luckily, there's a test to figure out whether or not you've got the chops to be creative in Corporate America:

Question 1: Have you ever had an idea, no matter how big or small, on how to improve a process, system, or product?

That's the only question.

If you answered yes to that question, congratulations! Your contributions are needed at your job.

I don't care if you weren't hired to do that. I don't care if you're not a graphic designer. I don't even care if you can't put together a slide deck. Successful creativity is, at its core, the ability to generate an idea and bring it into reality.

Ooh, that was good. I'm going to say it again in bold.

Successful creativity is, at its core, the ability to generate an idea and bring it into reality.

Do not bring problems to your boss. Bring solutions.

Do not bring complaints to your boss. Bring workarounds.

Do not bring up what is wrong. *Fix* what is wrong.

Here's how I pretty much doubled my salary in only 2 years of working for a company. Try this exercise yourself. I can't promise the money, but I can promise an improvement in your life:

Step 1: Write down a list of issues you or your co-workers face at least once a week.

Step 2: Write down a 5 solutions to each one of those problems. A solution is something that saves either time or money.

Step 3: Implement the easiest solution

Step 4: You are now a visionary. Rake in any money and/or admiration that comes your way.

Do you want to know a dirty little secret to this process? *Your idea doesn't have to be the best idea ever.* Assuming you have to think of the greatest idea ever is the best way to cripple yourself.

Your new solution just has to be better than what you have. Any improvement, no matter how big or small, is always rewarded either with actual money or imaginary reputation points (which I'm starting to think are even more valuable).

Creativity is the cure for the corporate crawl.

It's time to start doing your part.

Not-So-Magic Tactics; Magic Results

Here's something you might have noticed – What I write about isn't sexy. It doesn't make many guarantees. I'm not a get-rich-quick kind of guy.

My whole goal, really, is to help you set up a practical, sustainable lifestyle where you can enjoy what you do and minimize risk at the same time.

But maybe you don't enjoy what you do right now. Maybe you're tied up doing something for a "boss," but you dream of breaking out on your own.

There's a great way to get traction for a side hustle even while employed. It's not pretty. It's not always fun. It's not even guaranteed to work every time. Ready? Here it is:

Work for free.

Awful, right? I told you it wasn't very glamorous. But let me ask you this - if you have a job giving you steady paychecks, what's the harm in doing a little extra work? Not everything has to come with dollar bills attached.

Think about the last time you got a present unexpectedly. How did you feel? Loved? Impressed? Surprised? Maybe you even feel like you "owe" that person something.

These are all potential emotions you can transfer to people whenever you give them work for free. They will almost always pay you back in loyalty*, if not dollar bills.

*Important note: If you give with the expectation of getting something back, the whole system breaks down. Giving someone a present AND your expectations isn't really a "free" gift, is it? *

With that in mind, try these 4 free work tactics which I've used in my own Creative journey (from most to least effective in my experience)

Tactic #1: Offer to guest post/sing/star on someone else's site
Benefit: New Relationships

This is the oldest trick in the book, and despite the claims that "guest posting is dead," this is still my favorite tactic. It's probably not for the reason you think.

Most people believe a guest post will bring them a host of new readers, and while that may be true for some people, it's a small percentage.

The biggest value in doing this for me has been connecting with other site owners in my field.

The first person I did a guest post for built me a website for free, designed the cover of this book, and we stay in touch regularly.

The second person I did a guest post for shares my post almost every weekend.

The third person I did a guest post for is now working with me to plan out his book launch.

How many new readers did I get from these blog posts? I have no idea. But I got something better than readers – I got new friends.

The more new people in your world, the better, especially if those people are already doing something you want to be a part of.

Tactic #2: "Swag Bomb" Celebrities
Benefit: Exposure

This one is soooo much fun because here's the deal - most people in the public eye love themselves. There's nothing wrong with that. Part of the reason they have so much influence in the first place is because they believe the world can benefit from what they have to say.

People who love recognition also love the idea that someone is listening. I got picked to be on a popular web show (and showed up on thousands of people's radar) amongst a flood of submitted questions because I:

a) Specifically quoted something the host said on the show before

b) Went the extra mile to do something creative (which makes his show more interesting)

c) Came up with a question he'd never been asked before (which forces him to add more content to the show)

You can follow the same steps. To make them more generic, here's this formula:

a) Decide how to stroke the ego of the person you're trying to reach (they love to be known, remember?)

b) Do something creative and cool (write a poem, make a quote card, T-shirt, etc.)

c) Make sure it's not something they get all the time (don't just send an email that says "You're so great!")

Marc Ecko (of Ecko Clothing) did a phenomenal job of this. Whenever he was trying to get his brand off the ground, he tailored a personalized sweatshirt for Spike Lee and sent it to his mailbox. Spike wore it, talked about it, and now you see Ecko brand clothing all over the place.

Swag Bombs are powerful.

Tactic #3: Privately Rebrand Companies
Benefit: Practice

This is one I do all the time as well. It is toward the bottom of the list because usually, nobody sees what I do for other companies. I do it solely to keep my idea muscle in shape.

And you don't have to be a graphic designer for this. I'm not. I do LOVE to write headlines and taglines, though. Whenever I get bored, I'll sometimes pick out a local business and think up some taglines.

I do this a lot in my Micro Journaling practice. At the top of the page I'll list a business, either local or global, and make up taglines for them.

If you are a designer or photographer, you have an even clearer way of doing this - create a new logo, new stock photos, or a new website for the business in question. What if Twitter used a dolphin for their logo? How would you make that happen? What would it look like? How would you incorporate the new animal into the existing design?

Bonus Points: If you do this for a local business, you could actually just send them the mockup. Say in the email: "Hey there! This may sound odd, but I was thinking about your business, and I came up with some ideas around it. Feel free to take a look at these and use any you want."

Worst case scenario? You hear no response and your feelings might get a little hurt.

Best case scenario? They pay you for your ideas or hire you.

Not such a bad tactic after all. (If you remember Hannah from the *Discover* section, this should sound pretty familiar)

Tactic #4: Build a Personal Site
Benefit: Discipline

THE CREATIVE'S CURSE

This is the last on the list, but the first one people usually run to. I have a problem with people pouring all their effort into a personal site with no previous experience *or* audience because of this scenario that I've seen approximately 100 bazillion times:

Step 1: Johnny Blogger finally sets up his own website. YAY!

Step 2: Excited as all get out, Johnny posts something every day and shares it on social media.

Step 3: Surprisingly, no traffic magically comes knocking.

Step 4: Discouraged, Johnny gives up, wondering why nobody loves him.

Poor Johnny didn't have to go through that. Yes, there is still a big reason to have a personal site. Yes, it can still make you money and connections down the road.

But it also takes longer than all of these other tactics.

If you have no expectations on any of these other strategies (which you shouldn't), you should have even *less* for your personal site.

Starting a blog right now is like chucking a rock into a lake. You won't see much after the first ripples fade.

The only way to make an impact on that lake is by throwing thousands of rocks in the same spot for at least a year or so, when a little rock island starts to peek over the water.

It's the same with personal blogging.

At point of writing, I haven't earned a single dime from my personal site (that's changed if you're reading this ;), but I have earned a WHOLE lot of discipline.

There is value in showing up every day, even (especially) if nobody is looking. A personal site can teach you to do that.

[Author's note: If you are interested in more magic tactics, you'll find them in my 2nd book – The Unstoppable Creative – which takes a deeper dive into concrete strategies for career and business growth as a creative professional.

You can get that here: toddbrison.com/unstoppable]

Don't BS just because you can

There is a strange phenomenon which accompanies mastery of a craft. The "master" starts to feel the urge to phone it in.

To write pretty words that sound nice but mean nothing.

To take good pictures with no soul and use your name to give them attention.

To paint things which are beautiful just because you have the skills to.

To make animations which exceed *their* standards, but not yours.

I imagine this happens in every career, you know, a sort of settling in. I see James Patterson come out with 14 novels a year and wonder how many of them have ghost writers or if he suddenly became an expert in the Young Adult, Sci-Fi, and Romance Genre.

Coasting on your name alone has never worked, and it will never work.

Keep in mind, this is not a discussion of fans saying "this isn't as good as her old stuff!' No, this is strictly about you.

Whether or not *you* are giving up.

Whether or not *you* are cruising on your reputation and your past work alone

Whether or not *you* are continuing to do what you did when you were nobody - **pound the pavement, ride an idea deep into the night, create from the heart and bleed from the soul.**

The best artists aren't afraid to try new things. They aren't afraid to dramatically shift from everything they've done in the past and throw out something different. I wonder if they know, intuitively, that people would get tired of the same old same old. Because, by the way, they do.

What was once shocking will become average. What was once your ticket to recognition will become commonplace.

Do not sit with Complacency.

Dance with the Muse.

The Creative vs. The Businessman

The Creative seeks approval.
The Businessman seeks results.

The Creative is attached to his art.
The Businessman is removed from it.

The Creative operates on emotion.
The Businessman operates on logic.

To the Creative, money clouds the process.
To the Businessman, money *is* the process.

The Creative makes magic.
The Businessman makes metrics.

The Creative responds to people.
The Businessman responds to trends.

The Creative craves isolation.
The Businessman craves connections.

The Creative thinks in color.
The Businessman: Black and white.

The Creative would work for free, but
The Businessman demands a price.

The Creative is a dreamer.
The Businessman, a practitioner.

Ideas fuel The Creative.
Execution fuels the Businessman.

The Creative just wants to be happy.
The Businessman wants the same.

All successful creatives find a balance between these two extremes. It's up to you to find yours.

The Success Monster Part 1 - What to do After Your Post Goes Viral

It all started so innocently at first.

The extra-long walks.

The stretched-out lunches.

The "work is so crazy right now."

They were signs of a voice I've battled before. One who threatens all not-yet-successful people.

I one wrote a post on Medium that got big. Really big. Like "wait, did you guys confuse me for James Altucher or some other famous author?" big. I was three spots below Gary Vaynerchuck for top story of the day. Ten spots below the CEO of AirBnb.

This is what we Internet creatives live for right? The attention. The viral potential. The home run. The reach we could have never achieved even 10 years ago.

I thanked people on Twitter, responded to everyone who left a note. Said thank you, thank you, thank you, and then watched my numbers grow.

The rush of going viral (even semi-viral) is addictive. That's why we're all here, isn't it?

What people don't talk about is the next step. What happens after you hit that peak point and the numbers slow down? What happens when people stop drinking from that particular well?

The Rebound begins to speak:

> *"That was the best thing you've ever written... now your career is finished."*

It wasn't my first encounter with the beast. In college I wrote a sports piece which did very well around campus. Everywhere I went, people were giving me thumbs up. I got dozens of comments on Facebook.

I was so proud of myself.

Then I promptly wrote ABSOLUTELY NOTHING for four months. Not a single sentence.

Each time I would sit down to type, the voice of The Rebound would speak:

> *"Why bother? You won't do anything better than that."*

Confused and convinced he was right, I would close my laptop and dive into something much safer... like television or schoolwork.

THE CREATIVE'S CURSE

The Rebound that accompanies success is much, much, MUCH louder than the one which accompanies failure. We expect failure.

We don't expect success, so we don't know what to do with it.

Here's what to do with it:

Love the work. Not the result.

If you love the work, you will find a way to write another song, to design another piece, to come up with another idea.

If you love the work, you'll get back in the chair, you'll pull out your guitar, your camera, or your paintbrush.

If you love the work, you'll kick The Rebound in the face and chase the muse, no matter where she goes.

If you love the work, creation beats affirmation.

Every.

Single.

Time.

Break the Rules

I try to break the rules of art as much as possible.

Not because I have some rebellious streak inside me. Quite the opposite actually. I was "the good kid." My nature is to obey the road signs, listen to people in authority, and most importantly "do as I'm told."

While these things may never leave me (I was a child of two teachers, after all), I'm conscious to push back whenever I get the chance.

If you only do what other people tell you to do, you will not create the things they never dreamed of.

Everything you're looking at right now didn't exist at one point. Once upon a time, two guys decided to come up with the perfect chair. They put all their time and effort into making a structurally sound chair, one employees could sit in all day without injury or discomfort. There was just one problem – the chair was ugly as sin. The two men were told by multiple investors to come back when they had an "aesthetically pleasing" version of the chair.

They didn't listen. The chair was further engineered until it became ergonomically perfect.

THE CREATIVE'S CURSE

You've seen this chair. You may even be sitting in one right now because that chair (or a knock off of it), now sits in nearly every single corporate office in the world.

That didn't happen because the creators followed the rules.

They questioned the status quo. They moved beyond what was and saw what could be, even what *should* be.

This is the Creative's Curse - to push past what *is* and run the opposite direction.

The Success Monster Part 2 - Until You Connect, You Are Nobody

You know the one big post you wrote?

The one that everyone shared?

And hearted?

And "liked?"

And retweeted?

I have to tell you a little secret about those people.

They have no idea you wrote it.

People share ideas first. The Creative behind the art is an afterthought. They don't realize you are an actual human being, slaving away at every detail, trying 45 different colors until you get the right one, penning 17 different headlines until you find one that "feels right."

Until you reach out after they share.

Until you connect, you are an idea, not a person. Until you reach out and say, "Hey Jerry, thanks for liking my work" that person has no idea you exist.

THE CREATIVE'S CURSE

I need to share a dirty little secret at this point – when I started getting some big hits, one in particular, that got shared on Twitter a lot, do you know what I wanted to do when I saw people using my handle?

I wanted to ignore it.

Not because I wasn't grateful. Not because I didn't see it. Not because I just forgot.

I wanted to ignore tweets from a stranger sharing my work because I *wanted to seem too busy.*

Think about how ludicrous this line of thought is: I spent all this time and energy and work to get a post that went mildly-viral, and whenever it did, my ego got enormous.

"Look at us!" it said. "We're faaaamous!!"

Wrong.

Certainly that post was famous. It got shared hundreds of times across dozens of mediums. The post was a big deal. But I wasn't.

So I connected. I said thank you. I responded. Every single time. At midnight. On my lunch break. At 3 A.M.

To everyone.

Some of them never said anything back, and that's fine. But some of them did. Now some of them follow me for me, not just for what I write, but because they've realized I'm a human being.

A few of them I've really connected with. Not just moment-to-moment interactions that happen on the Internet, but "lifetime friends" kind of connected.

After all, isn't that what being a Creative is all about?

THE CREATIVE'S CURSE

Read these words whenever the momentum slows

When the heat cools,

When the traffic stops,

When people stop caring,

When your "fans" disappear,

When that blog post is a dud,

When you disappear in a mountain of new Internet "stuff."

You are more than just one thing.

Your career does not hinge on one piece of work.

It is the sum of a body of work.

You can always make another one.

You can always make another one.

I promise. You can always make another one.

The Success Monster Part 3 - The Irony of Creative Victories

The temptation, of course, is to copy success.

To pick apart the dos and don'ts of what works, to get your information directly from an article called "7 Steps to a Killer Blog Post," to pull out the pieces you know will be hits and Frankenstein them into something which has the highest likelihood to go viral.

If the goal of your work is to get attention, you have already lost. There will never be enough shares to satisfy.

We have enough people on the Internet who are cranking out "content" because they know it works to drive business right now. They know if they come up with "12 Ways to Life-Proof Your Garage," someone will read it. A percentage of those readers will stay, and a percentage of *those* readers will spend money.

It's a simple formula for a businessman.

But you are not just a businessman.

Do not create *content*. Create art.
Do not create like a business man. Create like a human being.

Do not create with your brain. Create with your soul.

If you want to *move* people, not merely put them into a sales funnel, turn your brain off and your heart on. Each piece is a new creation, a new start, a new mark on the world.

You really can hack the system if you want to. You can turn the Internet on its head and reverse-engineer your way to some kind of career.

Please don't.

"Your work doesn't appeal to everyone"

Of course it doesn't.

The more fame you achieve, the more criticism comes in.

The more criticism comes in, the more pressure you will feel to water down your message.

And then the agents start. And then your publicists start.

They want the best for you, and by "the best for you" that means "they want to sell more of your stuff to more people."

It's a natural human tendency to want more, but the answer to great art is almost never in more. Stuff of the heart doesn't scale well. It takes time and effort and emotion.

Always.

The Success Monster Part 4 - What Happens After Your Dreams Come True?

Fear of success is not altogether unfounded.

Consider J.K. Rowling, creator of Harry Potter.

She sweated and worked and bled and cried to bring young Harry into the world. She cut class and spent time in the library. She gave everything she had to make her dream come true.

And then one day, *it happened*. After getting what she described as "loads of rejections," Rowling finally got picked up by an agent, and the rest is history.

Rowling is 50 years old at time of writing.

What is she supposed to do for the rest of her life?

The creator of one of the most famous heroes of our time now has to live the next 40 or so years knowing that she will probably never write anything nearly as successful. She will likely never change the world like she did with Harry.

In fact, it probably took her a while to even enjoy writing again. When she finally did take a stab at a new story, here are some of the reactions she got to *The Casual Vacancy*:

> *"This novel was a major disappointment. My recommendation, if you feel you absolutely must read it, is to borrow it from your public library. Do not spend the money on this one."*

> *"The main problem with this book is that the most interesting character physically leaves the scene in the first chapter, and by the time you finish dragging yourself through the painful ordeal of completing the book, you'll feel that he's the luckiest one of all."*

> *"The Casual Vacancy is a dull and dismal book, about dull and dismal people living in a dull and dismal village."*

Ouch.

Imagine, if you will, a scenario where what you want most comes true. You change the world with an outstanding success, and millions of people adore your work. What would you do the very next day?

The destiny of a Creative has to be more than just writing a hit. It has to be more than filling bookstore shelves or making millions. And we need to talk about this now, so you can do away with your fear of success once and for all.

Here are a few things Rowling does:

1. Continue to do work she loves
After the shocking results of *The Casual Vacancy*, Rowling probably decided she was going to have to leave that pen name behind. Although she could have thrown in the towel and pursued another career, she knew writing was her true love.

Remember how Creatives get to reinvent themselves whenever they want? Rowling became Robert Gilbreath, and dove into the murder-mystery genre.

Money, after a while, fails to have meaning. Fame becomes fickle.

Loving the work for the work's sake is critical.

2. Pay it forward
Lumos is a charity which helps underprivileged children find families.

Money is only leverage, it's a tool (have I beat that drum enough yet???). Rowling has taken that tool and created something beautiful. She's given back to the world that gave her so much.

Giving is one of the best ways to keep life in perspective. By creating a foundation which changes lives, Rowling not only improves the world, she uses the cause to keep her head on straight.

P.S. Don't wait until you're rich to give things away. I'm not going to turn this into a sermon, but giving regularly completely changed my mindset around money. Most of the time, you can find someone who needs $50 a whole lot more than you do.

3. Grow what you've created

On July 8, 2014 the Internet exploded.

For the first time in 2007 there was news about Harry Potter. After 7 years, Rowling took to Potterwatch and released a brief story about Harry's whereabouts. With a simple gesture, she spread a wave of joy across Potterdom.

How many bands do you think hate their biggest hits? How many artists think what is most popular is their least favorite work?

The best work (especially in the Internet era) lives *forever*. Don't be afraid to revisit what's worked for you.

THE CREATIVE'S CURSE

You may never sell around 450 million copies like Rowling has, but if you do this Creative thing long enough, you receive some sort of success you didn't expect.

You better have a clear path of what to do with it.

You Will Never Hear These 4 Words Enough.

It's safe to say my writing career, this book, or even these words you're reading right now would not exist if I hadn't been told time and time again the words I'm about to tell you:

You can do it.

Yes, you, with your doubts and your fears and your inadequacy. Yes, you, who up until this point may have been too afraid to try lest you fail, too afraid to leap lest you fall. Yes, you, human.

You can do it.

The arena is noisier than ever. You will have to cut through a lot of trash. Artists are appreciated little, and can often be paid even less.

You can do it.

No, you do not have the ability to do it overnight. No, you will not gain a huge following in days or months or probably even a year. No, you do not have enough talent yet. No, there are not "10 Easy Ways" there.

But you can do it.

THE CREATIVE'S CURSE

Even after you start to be successful, people will doubt you. Some will openly mock you for no other reason than they are ashamed of their own shortcomings. Some will leave you.

But you can do it.

I read once that there are two types of artists in the world: Those who succeed and those who quit.

You can do it.

Read these words 100 times. Read them every day. Say them to yourself when you are sitting in the pit of self-doubt. Recite them when you feel like a fraud. And you will often feel like a fraud.

You can do it.

When your very biology is crying out that you stop, that you stay safe, that you need more sleep, that you should get a secure job, ignore it and go on.

Because you can do it.

If you promise not to listen to anyone who tells you the route to being an artist is easy, that you are only a couple clicks away from fame and fortune, I will promise to tell you this truth as often as I can.

Being an artist sucks sometimes. It is not something I wish on anyone who wasn't born into the world with the quiet but persistent suspicion they were meant to change it.

You can do it.

It's not easy. But you can do it.

Love, Feel, Cry

Those words all make the list of things we big manly men agreed to say as little as possible. For the curious, we also aren't supposed to say things like:

"Meghan Trainor's album is so good!" (even though it is)

and

"Pedicures are amazing" (even though they are)

But Creativity at the deepest level, and I mean the real stuff, not just a list with gifs any robot could have cranked out, comes from the heart.

It comes from pain and joy. It comes from laughter and sorrow. It comes from gut-wrenching sadness and brain-tickling pleasure.

It comes from the *experience* of life, not just the knowledge of it.

Most of these experiences start to level out after a certain age. It's easy to trudge through every year you live past 22 without bothering to actually notice anything that happens. Why do you think young adult novels are so popular?

TODD BRISON

Without intention, life becomes a white noise, with us flipping pages off the calendar like we'll get those days back.

We won't get them back.

Success makes life easier, that's for sure.

It's too bad great art doesn't come from an easy life.

FOR THE THINGS THAT ARE IMPOSSIBLE TO CAPTURE:

The sunset,
The sunrise,
The star-punctured night sky,
The first time she looks at you,
The loved one gone much too soon,

The hurt of a break up,
The youngest in make-up
The voice of your mother,
The kiss of a lover,
The cuddles in covers,
The warmth of others,
The bond of a brother,

The unfairness of life,
The pitch-black of night,
The deafening silence in the forest,
The crisp air in the morning,
The three children mourning,

The unfairness of death,
The father's last breath,
The grandma alone,

TODD BRISON

The non-ringing phone,
The hopeless dark evenings,
The smile and its angles
The prayers for an angel

For all of these things, you simply must try.

Maybe

Maybe you should just stay in line, work really hard at a job for someone else.

Maybe you should ask someone to tell you what to do.

Maybe you should pack up your pens and go get a life.

Maybe you should realize being creative just isn't worth it.

Maybe you should just chase the money.

Maybe you should become another copy.

Maybe you should become another copy.

Maybe you should do what your brother-in-law does. He's responsible, you know.

Maybe you should join the assembly line.

Maybe you should stop typing.

Maybe you should put up the brushes.

Maybe you should come to terms with the fact your art sucks.

Maybe you should realize nobody cares what you do.

Maybe you should keep your ability a secret.

Maybe you should leave it on a shelf.

Maybe you should grow up. Art is for children, after all.

Maybe you should keep your real job.

Maybe you should quit pretending.

Maybe you should stop with the imagination, already.

Maybe you should admit *They* are right.

Maybe you don't have what it takes.

But then again,

Maybe you do.

Acknowledgements

When I started this book, I had two thoughts in mind:

1. "Writing a book won't be that hard, it's just like blogging only more!"
2. "I don't even need anyone else!"

Both these thoughts were woefully wrong.

Kate: You laced up your smock and marched to a job you hated day after day to put food on the table because I was buried in my laptop, pursuing the ridiculous dream of becoming a writer. I will never forget that sacrifice, never undervalue your presence, and never stop pursuing a life for us both to thrive. Without you, honestly, I'd probably still be sitting in some dorm room catching up on The Simpsons. I love you.

Declan: You've mentioned before your book wouldn't exist without me. I think it's fair to say at this point – this book wouldn't exist without you. Thank you for calling me on my junk, reminding me of the details I never remember (like uploading this file to Amazon), and nudging me in the right direction. You,

Henry, and Erica are an excellent reminder to keep work in perspective.

Mom and Dad: For all the seemingly insignificant smiles, hugs, kisses, high-fives, milkshakes, life lessons, tears, laughter, movie nights, Sunday mornings, Saturday nights, rounds of golf, games of cards, carpools, extra classes, love, hope and guidance – thank you. You told me I could do whatever I wanted. It's not your fault I was crazy enough to believe that.

Ian: You're wrong. Hamilton is a genius musical, and not one bit "mediocre slam poetry." Other than that opinion, I can't imagine having a better younger brother.

Notes and Selected Further Readings

I got the idea for The Creative's Curse much like any writer does these days – it started as a post which got a lot of attention, and bloomed into a structure.

In no particular order, here are a few books which helped me along the way:

The Choose Yourself Series – James Altucher: I give away copies of these books as often as I can. It helped me change my paradigm and figure out how to move forward instead of waiting for a publisher to pick me.

The Millennial Way – Declan Wilson: This book was an eye-opener as well. Declan tells incredible stories and reminds us life isn't always about money, fame, or doing things how everyone thinks they should be done.

Moment Maker – Carlos Whittaker: More than an author, Carlos (Los) moved me with this piece. He helped me get my head out of the clouds and remind me although dreams are important, moments are better.

About the Author

Todd is an author who helps creative people find their untapped potential. He loves his redhead, Chacos, sweet potatoes, and writing until an urgent pull reminds him he hasn't peed in several hours.

He's been featured in CNBC, New York Observer, Inc. Magazine, and Apple News.

Most of his life is contained at toddbrison.com. The rest of it is in an old shoebox you'd have to come to his house to see.

One Last Thing...

Hey it's Todd here.

If you enjoyed this book or found it useful I'd be grateful if you posted a short review on Amazon. Your support makes a difference and I read all the reviews personally.

If you'd like to leave a review, please follow the link below to the book's page on Amazon:

https://amzn.com/b01ggpdly4

Thanks again for your support!

Other Books by the Author:

The Unstoppable Creative

Toddbrison.com/unstoppable

Made in the USA
Lexington, KY
01 September 2019